What's

Fig Leaves?

CHRISTIAN
FOCUS

With impressive thoroughness and depth, Heather examines modesty from a biblical, historical, and practical perspective. Mix in plenty of heart and grace, and you have a substantive, helpful resource for teachers, leaders, mentors, parents, and pastors who find themselves dealing with this complex and important subject.

Nancy DeMoss Wolgemuth

Author, Teacher/host for *Revive Our Hearts* radio

I enjoyed this book because it led my thinking about modesty into '*uncharted territory*'. This book is a blessing because of the author's extensive research, careful thought, wise humility, and her desire to be biblical and God-honoring. May it be used to glorify God in all who read it!

Kent Keller

Co-author of *Modesty: More than a Change of Clothes*

Associate pastor of Faith Bible Church

Sharpsburg, Georgia

What's up with the Fig Leaves?

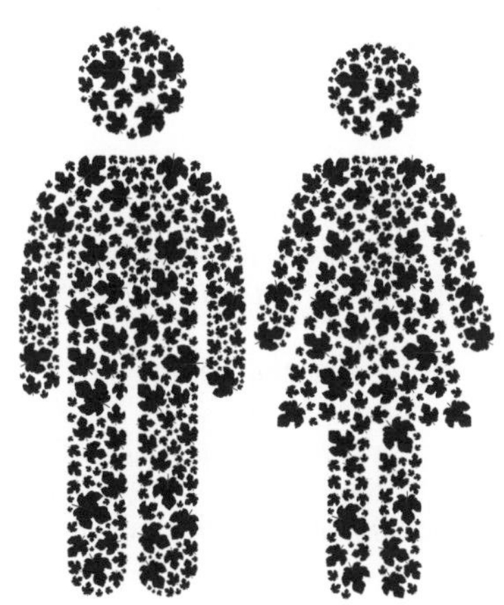

The Principles and Purposes of Modesty Uncovered

Heather Thieneman

Heather Thieneman lives in Kentucky where she is a writer and the archives office coordinator at a private academy. She is a member of Reformed Baptist Church of Louisville and has a love for missions and missionaries which has taken her to many places around the world.

paperback ISBN: 978-1-78191-772-5
epub ISBN: 978-1-78191-885-2
mobi ISBN: 978-1-78191-886-9
10 9 8 7 6 5 4 3 2 1

Published in 2016
by
Christian Focus Publications Ltd,
Geanies House, Fearn,
Ross-shire, IV20 1TW, Scotland.
www.christianfocus.com

Cover design by Pete Barnsley, Creative Hoot

Printed by Bell and Bain, Glasgow

CONTENTS

1: Modesty: A Ship in Distress

> 'The cry of "Breakers ahead!"' writes Alan Gurney 'was the first warning that the navigating officers had made a dreadful mistake in their dead reckoning....'
>
> 'Minutes later, in the howling dark of an autumn night, four ships of a Royal Navy fleet were mastless hulks being pounded to pieces between the hammer blows of the Atlantic breakers and the anvil of the Scilly Islands' granite reefs. Some two thousand men and officers...died on that night of October 23, 1707.... [a tragedy which] is still considered the worst shipwreck disaster ever suffered by the Royal Navy.'[1]

What could have caused such a disaster? Was it a depressed captain bent on self-destruction? Was it crewmen who were grossly incompetent? Was it just a little carelessness? Upon investigation it was found to be none of these. Those at the helm knew well the dangers of the Scilly Islands and were carefully steering clear of them. Yet somehow they crashed on the reefs they thought they were avoiding.

---

1. Alan Gurney, *Compass: A Story of Exploration and Innovation* (New York: W.W. Norton & Company, 2004), pp. 19-20.

In his book, *Compass: A Story of Exploration and Innovation*, Gurney gives three explanations for this tragedy: mistaken charts, an unknown current, and faulty compasses.

- The charts they were using showed the Scilly Islands miles north of their true location, causing the officers to think danger was further away than it really was.
- There was also an, as yet, undocumented current, now called the Rennell Current, pushing everything in its path north towards the islands, so that they didn't realize how fast they were approaching danger.
- Lastly, and most critically, were their compasses. The problem certainly wasn't a lack of them – between the ships of the fleet they had 145 – but when the compasses were later taken out for examination, it was found that in the inclement conditions of the voyage all but three had ceased pointing true north.[2]

Could it be that we are facing a similar tragedy in our day? Are we making shipwreck on the shores of immodesty, not intentionally or even carelessly, but while thinking we are sailing safely along, never imagining how close danger is? Have we been lulled into a false sense of security by mistaken 'charts' on modesty, by an ignorance of the sinful currents in our own hearts pulling us imperceptibly toward danger and, above all, by faulty consciences, which have ceased pointing true north by our long voyage in this world?

If these things are so, and this book is written out of the belief that they are, what is to be done? How can we avoid shipwreck?

2. In addition to having faulty compasses, their ship logs also showed they were not accounting for compass variation, which Edmond Halley had written on and charted six years earlier.

The Bible doesn't draw us a chart demarcating where the sea of modesty ends and the cliffs of immodesty begin. God has not left us any prophets to speak where the Bible does not. What we need is to have our 'compasses,' our consciences, realigned. But how do we do that?

A short lesson in compasses is in order, because to understand what causes a compass to give an inaccurate reading, you have to understand the secret to how a compass works. Gurney writes: 'Lodestone, loadstone, magnetite, oxide of iron, Fe3O4 – all describe a dull, gray-black ore that can be found as an outcrop of stone above ground. This unattractive rock has remarkable characteristics. Not only will it attract iron but it can magnetize iron. It also exhibits polarity. A long, slim sliver of lodestone, if suspended at its middle by a thread, will align itself north and south. This same lodestone sliver, if stroked against a metal needle, will transfer to the needle the same characteristics. The stroker, in other words, will have produced a compass needle.'[3]

Because a compass needle is iron and not lodestone, it always has the potential of losing its magnetization and there were many things on a long voyage which could interfere with a compass's reliability: contact with gunpowder, damp storage conditions, loud noises like gunfire or thunder. The important thing was to have a lodestone on board. With a lodestone the needle could always be remagnetized and the compass could be made accurate again. Unhappily, this was the downfall of the ships sailing towards the English Channel on October 23, 1707 – despite having 145 compasses onboard they were without even a single lodestone.

Like a lodestone, only God's Word points infallibly north; therefore it is only as our consciences are stroked with God's Word

3. Gurney, *Compass: A Story of Exploration and Innovation*, p. 31.

that they will provide us with an accurate reading on modesty. The pages ahead will seek to realign our consciences with biblical truth so that we can stay the course in a world – and even a church – which is increasingly losing its bearings in relation to modesty. This is not a book, however, which will answer the 'hot' questions, such as how long a woman's skirt should be. The Bible does not spell out the specifics of modesty and I have not had, as Ellen White, a founder of the Seventh-day Adventist Church, claimed to have had, a vision showing me how long skirts should be[4]. I believe in the sufficiency of the Word of God, in this case, that whatever God has revealed about modesty is sufficient to guide us in dressing modestly. James Spiegel, in the aptly named book *How to Be Good in a World Gone Bad*, wrote concerning modesty, 'Hard and fast rules in this area are, of course, hard to come by, but at least we should be thinking critically in this area, scrutinizing the choices we make about our attire and behavior. Developing critical awareness is more than half the battle in the pursuit of modesty.'[5] We will not, then, spend so much time on what is modest, as on what modesty is, for the better we understand the principles behind modesty, the better we will discern which clothes are consistent with those principles.

Understanding modesty requires addressing both the heart and the mind. The heart and the mind are far more connected

---

4. Ellen White claimed to have had a vision in the 1860s where she was shown some skirts which were somewhere between 8 to 10 inches from the floor. She wasn't sure exactly which it was so she chose 9 inches for uniformity's sake and sought to make it a rule among Seventh-day Adventists. This rule caused so much strife and division that eventually she said that the vision had just been for herself personally and not meant for others to follow (see *What's in your Clothes Closet?* by Dwight Arthur Delafield (Review and Herald Publishing, 1974), p. 62.)

5. James S. Spiegel, *How to Be Good in a World Gone Bad* (Grand Rapids, MI: Kregel Publications, 2004), p. 140.

than many people realize: what we think influences how we feel and what we feel influences how we think. To put it another way: sin in our heart darkens our thinking and error in our minds deadens our heart. If we are to understand modesty, it is as important to have our hearts purified as it is to have our minds clarified. Much that is written on modesty focuses on the lust that immodesty can provoke so that immodesty is seen to be almost exclusively a problem for the viewer, however we will see that it can be equally a problem for the wearer. Dressing immodestly is seldom done in perfect innocence; there are sinful currents that cause a person to, even unknowingly, dress immodestly. These currents are just as important to deal with as the immodest dress itself for what is happening in the heart of an immodest person is less obvious, but just as serious, as what happens in the heart of the person who is lusting.

This book is written primarily with pastors, parents and women in mentoring roles in mind. Although they may not be the ones most often guilty of dressing immodestly, they are the ones most responsible for teaching modesty. Though these leaders may feel they know instinctively what is modest and immodest, the principles behind those instincts may not be so clear, making it hard to pass on to the next generation much more than a seemingly arbitrary list of do's and don'ts. Furthermore, when something more foundational is sought out, many unwittingly give teaching that undermines the very foundations of modesty. They end up bailing water with one hand while cutting holes in the bottom of the boat with the other, all the time feeling frustrated that they are working so hard yet sinking so fast.

In laying a solid foundation, we may at times focus on the obvious, yet mastering the elementary principles of modesty will go a long way in shedding light on the difficult questions. In this regard, it is like science. We may instinctively know that the faster something is moving, the greater its impact will be when it hits a wall, even if we can't explain the physics behind it. It may feel tedious and pointless to learn the scientific explanation to something that seems plain common sense, but the science behind it will come in handy when we come to areas that are not so common, not so readily apparent, not so instinctive. When we don't have the basics mastered, when we don't have a firm grasp of the whys, we will not be prepared to answer the hard questions.

As you read along you will find many quotes taken from secular sources – psychologists, sociologists, fashion historians and others. My purpose in quoting them is not to look up to them as authorities on modesty. They have all said far more things that were false than were true. I have sought to be selective in what I quote, including them only when I found what they said insightful and thought-provoking.[6]

This book, though dealing primarily with modesty in principle, which is equally true for men and for women, will, when it comes to applications, more often speak of the dress of women. I realize that this is a touchy issue and that it seems unfair to some. Let me first say that I completely believe that men also have a responsibility to dress modestly and that they do not always live up to that responsibility. This is a problem. However, it seems to me that an objective person has to realize that female immodesty in our day is a far bigger problem and this book reflects that reality. It's not that I have a double standard. It's that men generally do a better job, not a perfect job, it is true, but, overall, a better job of keeping to a reasonable standard of modesty than women do. I also believe that the Bible itself justifies such an approach since it deals more with women and

---

6. One of the things I found in my research was how many more secular books than Christian books there are on the subjects of modesty and dress.

their dress than it does with men and their dress. At one point I will seek to show that immodesty is especially, not exclusively, but especially, a female sin.

As I have read dozens of blogs on modesty and the hundreds of comments occasioned by those blogs, I have noticed that, no matter how well-balanced the post seems to me, there will be some who will feel the writer excused men and blamed women for lust. So let me state at the outset, unhesitatingly and unequivocally, that I believe that lust is first and foremost a problem with the heart of the one lusting. Immodest dress can tempt someone to sin, but it cannot force someone to sin and we are all responsible for our own actions regardless of what others around us do or wear.

Let me say it a different way: by dressing modestly we can prevent temptation, though not necessarily sin, whereas by guarding our minds we can prevent sin, though not necessarily temptation. This is to say that while a Christian can control and is responsible for what he wears, he cannot control, is not responsible for, what goes on in the minds of those who see him and it is also to say that a Christian can control and is responsible for what goes on in his mind even though he cannot control what people around him are wearing. These things mean that guarding our minds will more surely derail lust than getting everyone to dress modestly. This is an important point that I will try not to let us forget in our study of modesty.

However, in the end, this is a book on modesty in dress, not on lust, so it will spend much more time dealing with the mind, heart and actions of the one dressing immodestly than on the one lusting. If I were to write a book on the human eye, I would spend much more time dealing with the eye than I did with the heart. This would not mean that I believed that the eye was more crucial to the life of the body than the heart, it would only mean that

I had chosen the eye for my subject because I thought it was also important to understand. There are books, very good books, on dealing with lust. This is simply not meant to be one of them.

Perhaps one reason teaching on modesty has the potential to be so offensive is that those who have been most notable for championing it have often been marked by especially ugly sins – self-righteousness, legalism, hypocrisy, blame shifting – and, all too often, by especially advanced stages of these sins. Ever since the demon-possessed girl followed Paul around loudly commending his teaching it has been one of Satan's most effective strategies to disparage truth by putting it in the mouths of the most objectionable people. I confess I had second thoughts on writing this book when I read some of the mean-spirited and grossly imbalanced material out there on modesty by modern-day wolves in sheep's clothing. I don't want be identified with them or to give them anything they could use as ammunition. I feel sorry for those who have suffered under such teaching and I fear opening old wounds or causing confusion. Though I hope this will ultimately be a freeing, healing book, I realize that if you have been badly burned by unbiblical teaching on modesty this may be a painful book to read at times. May God give you comfort and encouragement and help you to see how lovely modesty can be when it is in the context of grace and love.

Before closing this chapter, let me change the analogy from compasses to something closer to home. Have you ever been driving with someone when the windshield fogged up so badly that the driver couldn't make out the road anymore? At that point, you as a passenger had two options. You could roll down your window, stick your head out and with your clear perspective start yelling out specific directions: 'Turn a little to the left, okay hold it, now a little to the right. Slow down to 25 mph, there's a curve coming up.' Or you could turn the defogger on to clear up the windshield so that the driver could see for himself. Taking this second option means that the driver may not make the exact decisions you would if you were at the wheel. He may take the curves a little faster than you think is prudent, he may hug the curb a little more than you're comfortable with, but if the driver has a heart to drive safely, he will stay on the road and out of the ditches. The objective of this book is to be a 'defogger' that will help you see for yourself and keep you out of ditches.

In order for this defogger to be effective it must be read prayerfully. To neglect to pray would be like turning on the defogger without turning on the fan. Not much is going to get cleared up. Read prayerfully because I am sure this book contains errors, I am far from infallible and so I am sure I am wrong at points, so pray that God would protect you from the errors and help you to avoid them. Read prayerfully because I trust it contains truth, I believe there are many things that are right, including some things that may at first seem uncomfortable and difficult, so pray that God would help you to embrace everything that is true. Above all, pray for the Holy Spirit's guidance. The Bible doesn't spell out the standards of modesty, God doesn't give prophetic visions to reveal the correct length of our skirts, but God has given His Spirit to lead and guide us into all truth. The more we lean on Him for help, the more we can hope to have our minds cleared up, even about things that now look foggy and confusing.

2: Fig Leaves: Then and Now

To begin to understand modesty, we have to go back to the beginning. Questions such as: *Where does modesty came from? Why are we ashamed to be seen naked in public? What is the purpose of clothing? Why are genitals especially in need of covering?* are best answered in the Garden of Eden:

> 'And they were both naked, the man and his wife, and were not ashamed....So when the woman saw that the tree was good for food, that it was pleasant to the eyes, and a tree desirable to make one wise, she took of its fruit and ate. She also gave to her husband with her, and he ate. Then the eyes of both of them were opened, and they knew that they were naked; and they sewed fig leaves together and made themselves coverings. And they heard the sound of the LORD God walking in the garden in the cool of the day, and Adam and his wife hid themselves from the presence of the LORD God among the trees of the garden. Then the LORD God called to Adam and said to him, 'Where are you?' So he said, 'I heard Your voice in the garden,

> and I was afraid because I was naked; and I hid myself.' And He said, 'Who told you that you were naked? Have you eaten from the tree of which I commanded you that you should not eat?... Also for Adam and his wife the LORD God made tunics of skin, and clothed them." (Gen. 2:25, 3:6-11, 21)

A. The Shame of Nakedness

John Calvin writes, 'That the nakedness of men should be deemed indecorous and unsightly, while that of cattle has nothing disgraceful, seems little to agree with the dignity of human nature.'[1] In other words, why is it that we who were made in God's image are ashamed to be seen publically naked when the beasts of the earth, from the littlest mouse to the mightiest lion, feel none of that shame?

It hasn't always been that way. In the beginning Adam and Eve felt no shame at their nakedness; it wasn't until after they ate the forbidden fruit that they felt shame, realizing, as if for the first time, that they were naked[2]. What brought about this change?

---

1. John Calvin, *Commentaries of the First Book of Moses Called Genesis* (Grand Rapids, MI: Baker Book House, 1996), p. 137.
2. In Chapter 2 of Genesis, the word translated naked is *'arom* and in Chapter 3 the Hebrew word *'erom* is used. Certainly in Chapter 2 the nakedness spoken of is innocent and in Chapter 3 the nakedness is guilty and shameful, however I cannot find any difference of meaning between the two words. They are both from the same root word and are used very similarly in the Old Testament. Frank E. Gaebelein believes that there is a difference in the meaning and that *'erom* has a connotation of judgment, citing its use in Deuteronomy 28:48 (see *The Expositor's Bible Commentary, Volume 2* (1990), pg. 49). However, *'erom* can also be used of innocent nakedness (Ezek. 18:7, 16) and *'arom* can be used of nakedness as a result of judgment (Hosea 2:3, Amos 2:16). Victor P. Hamilton agrees: 'there is no observable difference in meaning between the adjectives 'erom (3:7) and 'arom (2:25).' -*The New International Commentary on the Old Testament: The Book of Genesis Chapters 1–17* (Grand Rapids, MI: William B. Eerdmans, 1990), p. 191.

It wasn't that their bodies changed, suddenly becoming more ugly or embarrassing. It wasn't that another person came on the scene, it was still just Adam and Eve and God.

Sin entered the world, that's what happened[3]. We can say that so nonchalantly because we can't imagine what it would be like to be perfect and without sin, let alone a whole world perfect and without sin; we can't imagine what it would be like to go from perfectly happy and holy to profoundly wretched and wicked at the bite of an 'apple'. Fall is too nice, too well-behaved a word for such cataclysmic corruption; it was, without hyperbole, heart-breaking and earth-shattering. These new feelings of shame were the tip of the iceberg of indwelling sin birthed by the Fall. In retrospect, Adam and Eve's nakedness was the least of their problems; however, it was also a symbol, a picture, of their greatest problem.

Before we get to their greatest problem, and ours, let's look more at this correlation between nakedness and shame.[4] A Bible dictionary will tell you that the concepts of nakedness and shamefulness are so closely related that public nakedness is often

---

3. '[C]lothes came in with sin. We should have no occasion for them, either for defense or decency, if sin had not made us naked, to our shame.' –Matthew Henry on Genesis 3:21. '…in man's fallen state, a sense of shame relative to nakedness is entirely appropriate.' –Henry M. Morris in *The Genesis Record: A Scientific and Devotional Commentary on the Book of Beginnings,* (Grand Rapids, MI: Baker Book House, 1976), p. 130.

4. 'With the exception of this verse [Gen. 2:25], nakedness in the OT is always connected with some form of humiliation. The three major uses of nakedness are: (1) as a description of the poor (Job 24:7, 10; 31:19; Ezek. 18:16); (2) as a sign of shame or guilt (Gen. 3:7, 10, 11; Ezek. 16:22, 37, 39; Hosea 2:3; Amos 2:16; Micah 1:8); (3) in reference to birth (Job 1:21; Eccles. 5:15). A full documentation of all passages would show that nakedness as a symbol of guilt is most frequent….' –Victor P. Hamilton in *The New International Commentary on the Old Testament: The Book of Genesis Chapters 1–17* (Grand Rapids, MI: William B. Eerdmans, 1990), p. 181.

used figuratively to show shame and disgrace. It is especially used of Israel and the disgrace that God allows her to experience when she forsakes Him:

> 'I will lift your skirts over your face, I will show the nations your nakedness, and the kingdoms your shame.' (Nahum 3:5)
>
> 'Your nakedness shall be uncovered, yes, your shame will be seen.' (Isa. 47:3)
>
> '... All who honored her despise her because they have seen her nakedness...' (Lam. 1:8)
>
> 'Pass by in naked shame...' (Micah 1:11)

The idea of nakedness is also used to figuratively show the shame of the haughty Laodiceans:

> 'I counsel you to buy from Me gold refined in the fire, that you may be rich; and white garments, that you may be clothed, that the shame of your nakedness may not be revealed...' (Rev. 3:18)

Again in Revelation 16:15 nakedness is used figuratively to show shame:

> 'Behold, I am coming as a thief. Blessed is he who watches, and keeps his garments, lest he walk naked and they see his shame.'

Literal nakedness is said to be something that care must be taken to avoid exposing, even accidentally:

> 'Nor shall you go up by steps to My altar, that your nakedness may not be exposed on it.' (Exod. 20:26)
>
> 'And you shall make for them linen trousers to cover their nakedness; they shall reach from the waist to the thighs. They shall be on Aaron, and on his sons when they come into the tabernacle of meeting...' (Exod. 28:42-43)

Covering literal nakedness is a sign of respect and honor:

> 'But Shem and Japheth took a garment, laid it on both their shoulders, and went backward and covered the nakedness of their father [Noah]. Their faces were turned away, and they did not see their father's nakedness.' (Gen. 9:23)

> 'And those members of the body which we think to be less honorable, on these we bestow greater honor; and our unpresentable parts have greater modesty.' (1 Cor. 12:23)

Covering nakedness is a sign of love and protection:

> '... I spread My wing over you and covered your nakedness...' (Ezek. 16:8, see also vv. 7-14)

Uncovering nakedness is a sign of judgment:

> 'Because the daughters of Zion are haughty, and walk with outstretched necks and wanton eyes, walking and mincing as they go, making a jingling with their feet, therefore...the Lord will uncover their secret parts[5].' (Isa. 3:16-17)

> 'So shall the king of Assyria lead away the Egyptians as prisoners and the Ethiopians as captives, young and old, naked and barefoot, with their buttocks uncovered, to the shame of Egypt.' (Isa. 20:4)

---

5. The Hebrew word translated secret parts is *pothah* (this word is only used one other time in Scripture and that is in I Kings 7:50 where it is translated 'hinges' in a description of the temple) and *Strong*'s says it is from a word that means 'to open' and can be used of a hole, a hinge or the female pudenda. It is obviously that last meaning that is in view here, although this verse is speaking figuratively. This verse is talking about the Israelite people as if they were promiscuous women: the wanton eyes, the way of walking described as 'mincing' are all marks of a woman who is out to ensnare a man. Even promiscuous women seldom like to have their most intimate body part displayed before the public. No matter how shameless a woman may be, this part of her body is usually one she would be embarrassed to have stripped bare before the gawking stares of men.

Henry M. Morris well says, '...the shame of nudity is no artificial inhibition introduced by the conventions of civilization, as certain anthropologists and self-serving sophisticates have urged. It has its source in this primeval awareness of sin, and is only discarded when the moral conscience has been so hardened as to lose all sensitivity to sin.'[6] This is important because if there were no shame in public nakedness, then modesty would be a moot issue. It is true that most of these verses were speaking of nakedness symbolically, but the very reason something is used as a symbol is because it shares the same trait as the thing symbolized. Nakedness is used figuratively of shame because literal nakedness is shameful.

This brings us back to the bigger picture of Adam and Eve's shame, it brings us back to their real problem, of which their nakedness was only a picture. We are clued in that there is something more going on than shame at their physical nakedness by who their shame is directed towards. They are not hiding from each other, they are hiding from God.

God sees them. Their bodies and their hearts are naked before Him. Before the Fall, when they were perfect and God was perfectly delighted with them, when there was nothing to hide, nothing to be ashamed of, this had been a welcome thought. But, now, because of that one bite of forbidden fruit, sin has corrupted their heart, evil is lurking inside of them and the thought of God, the One who is of purer eyes than to look upon iniquity, seeing them is terrifying. And so they do what man has done ever since, they try to hide behind a covering of their own making.

---

6. Henry M. Morris, *The Genesis Record: A Scientific and Devotional Commentary on the Book of Beginnings*, (Grand Rapids, MI: Baker Book House, 1976), p. 116.

They first try to cover themselves by fastening together[7] fig leaves, possibly because they were the largest leaves they could find.[8] The Bible says that they used these fig leaves to make for themselves 'coverings.' The Hebrew word here translated coverings is from the word that means to gird. Sometimes it has been translated girdle, other translations have translated it apron, the best translation is probably loincloth; whatever one calls it, it was a piece of clothing which covered mainly the genitals.

Perhaps at first Adam and Eve feel that they have been made decent by their efforts. But then God comes. What looked sufficient to themselves when it was just them, now looks unbelievably inadequate when God comes on the scene and so they hide. Or they try to hide. But God finds them and deals with their sin, hinting at the time He will deal with it once and for all[9]. God also pities the inadequacy of their clothing and makes for them tunics of skin[10]. Here the word is not girdle, here it is a fairly generic word but one which indicates something more

---

7. 'And when they are said to sew these together, it is not to be supposed that they sewed them as tailors sew their garments together, since they cannot be thought to be furnished with proper instruments, or that they tacked them together with some sort of thorns, or made use of them instead of needles; but they took the tender branches of the fig tree with leaves on them, as the word signifies, see Nehemiah 8:15 and twisted them round their waists; which served for "girdles", as some render the word, and the broad leaves hanging down served for aprons…' –John Gill

8. 'The fig tree produces the largest leaves of any tree that grows in Palestine…' – Victor P. Hamilton in *The New International Commentary on the Old Testament: The Book of Genesis Chapters 1-17* (Grand Rapids, MI: William B. Eerdmans, 1990), p. 191.

9. See Genesis 3:15

10. 'By so doing God gave His approval of the sense of shame which had led our first parents to cover their nakedness...' – H. C. Leupold in *Exposition of Genesis Volume 1 Chapters 1-19* (Grand Rapids, MI: Baker Book, 1949), p. 178.

substantial, something that would cover the upper body as well as the lower body. The word translated tunics comes from a word meaning to cover, in other places it is translated coat, shirt, garment and robe. It is the same word used of Joseph's coat of many colors. Adam and Eve had felt their need, but they didn't grasp the magnitude of their need and so they thought they could deal with it themselves. But God shows them that no, their need of covering is far greater than they imagined and only He can cover their sins. As Albert Barnes put it in his commentary on Genesis, 'The coats of skin were a faithful emblem and a manifest guarantee of those robes of righteousness which were hereafter to be provided for the penitent in default of that original righteousness which he had lost by transgression.'

'Clothing,' Philip Eveson in a commentary on Genesis says, 'is a theme running throughout Scripture in connection with the essential truth of the gospel.'[11] Here are some examples:

> '...all our righteousnesses are like filthy rags...' (Isa. 64:6)

> 'Then He answered and spoke to those who stood before Him, saying, 'Take away the filthy garments from him.' And to him He said, 'See, I have removed your iniquity from you, and I will clothe you with rich robes.' (Zech. 3:4)

> 'I counsel you to buy from Me gold refined in the fire, that you may be rich; and white garments, that you may be clothed, that the shame of your nakedness may not be revealed.' (Rev. 3:18a)

> 'After these things I looked, and behold, a great multitude which no one could number, of all nations, tribes, peoples, and tongues, standing before the throne and before the Lamb, clothed with white robes, with palm branches in their hands.... Then one of the elders answered, saying to me, 'Who are these

11. Philip Eveson, *The Book of Origins: Genesis Simply Explained* [part of the Welwyn commentary series] (Darlington, England: Evangelical Press, 2001), p. 111.

> arrayed in white robes, and where did they come from?' And I said to him, 'Sir, you know.' So he said to me, 'These are the ones who come out of the great tribulation, and washed their robes and made them white in the blood of the Lamb.' (Rev. 7:9-14)

> 'I will greatly rejoice in the LORD,
> My soul shall be joyful in my God;
> For He has clothed me with the garments of salvation,
> He has covered me with the robe of righteousness...' (Isa. 61:10)

The text which illustrates this the most clearly:

> 'So those servants went out into the highways and gathered together all whom they found, both bad and good. And the wedding hall was filled with guests. But when the king came in to see the guests, he saw a man there who did not have on a wedding garment. So he said to him, "Friend, how did you come in here without a wedding garment?" And he was speechless. Then the king said to the servants, "Bind him hand and foot, take him away, and cast him into outer darkness; there will be weeping and gnashing of teeth."' (Matt. 22:10-13)

This truth was not lost on our hymn writers, many of whom used clothing to picture Christ's righteousness[12], most notably Nikolaus L. von Zinzendorf:

> 'Jesus, Thy blood and righteousness
> My beauty are, my glorious dress;
> 'Midst flaming worlds, in these arrayed,
> With joy shall I lift up my head.

---

12. See also Charles Wesley's 'And Can It Be', Edward Mote's 'My Hope Is Built on Nothing Less', Augustus Toplady's 'Rock of Ages' and Robert Murray McCheyne's 'When this Passing World Is Done'.

'This spotless robe the same appears,
When ruined nature sinks in years;
No age can change its glorious hue,
The robe of Christ is ever new.'

You may not have thought about it, but you have a witness to your need of Christ every morning. Would you want to leave for your day's activities without putting any clothes on? Of course not. Is not even the thought embarrassing? Wouldn't you rather do almost anything else? Where does that shame come from? Your pet doesn't share those feelings[13]. Your cat or dog would see clothes as the greatest annoyance. Why is it that to us – across cultures and across millennia – they are the greatest necessity? It's not a defect with our bodies, our bodies are fearfully and wonderfully made, more so than any of the animals and yet even rats don't blush to scamper around naked. Evolutionists have no explanation for it. Modesty reveals the fallacy of their theory for why should those who are more 'evolved' feel more shame than those who are less 'evolved'? The Garden of Eden alone provides our answer: shame at being publically naked is a picture of the shame we should feel at being spiritually naked before God and of our need to be clothed in the righteousness of Another. Every morning that we get dressed for the day should be a reminder to us of our need for Christ. Animals don't have this shame because animals don't have this need for Christ.

We also must not fool ourselves into thinking that we can sew together a few leaves of our own righteousness, as big as they

---

13. This has not escaped the notice of psychologists. Elizabeth Hurlock in *The Psychology of Dress* observes: 'The trait [modesty] is specifically a human one as no animal shows any signs of embarrassment, though totally unclothed, in the presence of other creatures.' – *The Psychology of Dress* (Ronald Press Company, 1929), p. 16. Evolution has nothing to account for this difference, only we as Christians have an explanation.

may seem to us, and be acceptable in the eyes of God. The Bible tells us that our own righteousness is as filthy rags (Isa. 64:6). If a gunman broke into your home spraying bullets, you wouldn't run to the laundry basket to protect yourself with some old dirty T-shirts. Yet that would be sanity compared to protecting yourself from God's justice with the dirty rags of your own good works. It doesn't matter how good your good works are any more than it mattered that Adam and Eve used the biggest leaves they could find. If there had been others to compare themselves to, perhaps a Mr. Shimrath down the street dressed in apricot leaves and a Miss Maachah who worked at the corner grocery sporting a skimpy olive leaf loincloth, Adam and Eve in their ample fig leaves would have come out looking pretty good. And, as it was, Adam and Eve did feel pretty well covered... until God arrived. In the light of God's holiness their indecency was more inescapable than that of someone stark naked in a crowd of burqa wearing Muslims.

Put ever so much time and effort into being good, succeed in your own eyes as much as you may, find the largest leaves you can, wrap yourself in as many dirty rags as you will, it will never be sufficient. Only Christ's righteousness is sufficient to cover our shame. Only Christ can give us a wedding garment. Our loincloths of self-righteousness may feel sufficient here on earth as we compare ourselves with our fellow Adams and Eves but when we stand in the presence of a thrice holy God, we will be left calling on the rocks and hills to hide us from the face of the Lamb. Only then it will be too late, there will not be a chance to ask God to make us a better covering. The better covering has already been made in the person of Jesus Christ and if we reject Him now there can await us nothing but the wrath of God.

Not only did Adam and Eve's efforts not mitigate their sin, it augmented their sin to think that they somehow could rectify their horrendous Fall by a few flimsy leaves. If Adam and Eve had instead run to God for mercy, who knows what would have happened, but we know today what happens when people run to God, casting off the dirty rags of their own goodness and throwing themselves on Christ's righteousness:

> 'I will greatly rejoice in the LORD,
> My soul shall be joyful in my God;
> For He has clothed me with the garments of salvation,
> He has covered me with the robe of righteousness…' (Isa. 61:10)

There may be people who pick up this book who are trusting in their own righteousness, perhaps even the righteousness of their own modest dress. Perhaps you were drawn to this book because you do take modesty seriously; it is to you a way to earn favor with God and acceptance into heaven. If so, my friend, keep reading because there is something you desperately need to know.

Our need for modesty is a symbol of the reality of our need for Christ's righteousness, but there is always a danger of revering the symbol while despising the reality. In the Old Testament many Jews trusted in their physical circumcision who were not circumcised in heart and the Bible tells us that that did them no good (Rom. 2:28-29, 1 Cor. 7:19, Gal. 5:6, 6:15). In our own day there are people who trust in their baptism who have not been spiritually raised to new life in Christ. Symbols are given to us to point us to the reality, when we use them to obscure the reality we are twisting them and turning what should be a blessing into a curse. Likewise, modesty cannot make us presentable in the eyes of God, it cannot hide the shame of our sin. Far, far, light years far, better to go around dressed in loincloths on our body than to go before God dressed only in the righteousness of our modesty.

To try to use modest dress as a means of earning our salvation is the worst perversion possible for not only are we despising Christ's righteousness in favor of our own, but we are twisting that which was meant to point us to Christ's righteousness and using it to despise Christ.

Maybe an analogy will help you understand the travesty of this. The American flag is only a symbol of America. It has no power of its own but it is honored by those who love America. Perhaps no one has hated America more than the 9/11 Al Qaeda operatives who flew planes into the World Trade Center. What they did was despicable and brings forth our indignation on its own. But what would we have felt if we had gone to their houses afterwards and found that they were flying the American flag? Or if we had found out that Osama bin Laden was singing the 'Star-Spangled Banner' while he watched the World Trade Center towers crumble? Far from mitigating their crime, it would increase it. To make a pretense of honoring the symbol while dishonoring what that symbol represents is to make mockery of it all. You might as well gain God's favor by draping a scarlet robe over Jesus' shoulders, putting a reed scepter in his right hand and a crown of thorns on his head, and then, after spitting on him, using his 'scepter' to beat his 'crown' down into his head until the blood runs down his face, all the while shouting 'Hail, King of the Jews!' as to gain God's favor by dressing modestly. While there is still time, reject the idea of earning God's approval by anything you do and flee to Christ, trusting only in His righteousness to make you right with God (see Rom. 3–5).

Others reading this may think that as long as they are trusting in Christ alone for salvation, it doesn't much matter what they think about modesty or how they dress. But this attitude is as worthy of contempt as those who claim to love America and yet insist it is their right to burn the American flag. If the thing itself is precious to you, its symbol should be precious to you. Furthermore, modesty is more than a symbol or a picture of something else, we will see that it serves important purposes and is a moral issue in and of itself.

B. Modesty and Sexuality

Now we come to the question, why did Adam and Eve cover their genitals? To us, that makes sense because it has been a part of the body that has been covered ever since by almost every, if not every, culture throughout history, but why did it make sense to them? After all, it was their hand that plucked the fruit and their mouth that ate it, so why didn't they cover their hands and their mouths? What was it about their sense of sin and shame which caused them to feel the need to cover their sexual organs?

The few commentators who deal with this question offer several explanations:

Frank E. Gaebelein thinks that they covered their genitals in order to hide their differences from one another.

> 'They were ashamed of their nakedness, and they sewed leaves together to hide their differences from each other.'[14]

Augustine thinks that before the Fall, Adam and Eve did not feel shame because their sexual organs could not be used to sin, shame entered when the possibility of using their sexuality in perverse ways entered.[15]

---

14. Frank E. Gaebelein, ed., *The Expositor's Bible Commentary, Volume 2* (Grand Rapids, MI: Zondervan Publishing House, 1990), p. 52.

15. [Before the Fall] 'they felt no shame, because no desire stirred their organs in defiance of their deliberate decision. The time had not yet come when the rebellion of the flesh was a witness and reproach to the rebellion of man against his Maker.' – Augustine, *City of God*, book 14, chapter 17, quoted in Andrew Louth, ed., *Ancient Christian Commentary on Scripture Genesis 1–11* (Downers Grove, IL: Intervarsity Press, 2001).

The Keil and Delitzsch Biblical Commentary on the Old Testament says that

> 'with the destruction of the normal connection between soul and body through sin, the body ceased to be the pure abode of a spirit in fellowship with God, and in the purely natural state of the body the consciousness was produced not merely of the distinction of the sexes, but still more of the worthlessness of the flesh; so that the man and woman stood ashamed in each other's presence, and endeavoured to hide the disgrace of their spiritual nakedness, by covering those parts of the body through which the impurities of nature are removed.'

Henry M. Morris thinks it was because 'the springs of human life had been poisoned.'[16] He writes,

> '...they realized that the very fountainhead of human life had now become corrupted by their disobedience and they became acutely aware of their nakedness. Their children would all be contaminated with the seed of rebellion, so that their feeling of guilt centered especially on their own procreative organs. The result was that they suddenly desired to hide these from each other, and from God.'[17]

Alan Dunn believes it was evidence of the death of their intimacy,

> '... they took fig leaves, with which they made neither earmuffs, nor sunglasses, nor party hats. They made loin coverings. They separated precisely at the point of their one-flesh intimacy. Physical intimacy gives expression to a full-orbed heart and soul intimacy. By their sin, they killed their intimacy, they

---

16. Morris, *The Genesis Record*, p. 104. This view is shared by the 18th century Bible commentator John Gill.

17. Morris, *The Genesis Record*, p. 115.

> murdered their union and intimacy's epitome expression was buried beneath a leaf.'[18]

The Bible doesn't tell us why Adam and Eve felt shame specifically regarding their sexual organs and it's risky to speculate where the Bible is silent, but let's take a few minutes to look at what we do know about nakedness and sexuality and perhaps in the light of what we do know, what we aren't told explicitly will become clearer.

First of all, we know that this was not an isolated happenstance. It's not just Adam and Eve who felt the need to cover their genitals, for the last 6000+ years mankind has felt the same need. There are few places where people do not feel some need to cover their sexual organs. Whatever else may or may not be covered, whatever the differences in standards of modesty, this one thing remains the same. There must be a reason for something that is so universal.

Second, we know that nakedness and sexuality often go hand-in-hand in the Bible. Leviticus 18 uses the term 'uncover nakedness' repeatedly to refer to intercourse. Seeing someone naked was a euphemism for having sex with them. We also see this connection between sexuality and nakedness in everyday life, in the fact that before a child is sexually aware he is often not embarrassed to be seen naked. This suggests that our sexuality, as well as our sinfulness, plays a role in the shame we feel at being naked. Adam and Eve as sexual beings before sin felt no shame at nakedness. The closest we can see their shame-freeness approximated in the world since then is in young children who, while sinful, have not yet blossomed in their sexuality.

---

18. Alan Dunn, *Gospel Intimacy in a Godly Marriage* (North Bergen, NJ: Pillar and Ground Publications, 2009), p. 38.

Third, we know that the Bible uses sexuality and marriage to picture God's relationship with His people. In the Old Testament God used this imagery of His relationship with Israel[19]:

> 'For your Maker is your husband...' (Isa. 54:5)
>
> 'And as the bridegroom rejoices over the bride, So shall your God rejoice over you.' (Isa.62:5b)

In the New Testament the imagery of marriage is used especially of Christ's relationship with the Church[20]:

> ' "For this reason a man shall leave his father and mother and be joined to his wife, and the two shall become one flesh." This is a great mystery, but I speak concerning Christ and the church.' (Eph. 5:31-32)
>
> '...Come, I will show you the bride, the Lamb's wife.' (Rev. 21:9b)

Kris Lundgaard writes, 'Marriage has always represented the spiritual intimacy of God with his people in love and kindness.'[21] Our sexuality, then, is special because what it represents is special. In this we see the amazing depths of the love God has for us and the joy He takes in us; God uses the climax of human pleasure to try to give us a glimpse of how He feels towards us! Justly the Bible calls it a mystery. If Solomon, the wisest man who ever lived and a man not lacking in sexual experience, found the way of a man with a maid too difficult to understand, how much more the way of God with His people?

> 'Tis mystery all: th' Immortal dies!
> Who can explore his strange design?

19. See also Isaiah 61:10; Jeremiah 2:2, 3:14, 20; Ezekiel 16:1-32; the Song of Solomon and the book of Hosea.

20. See also John 3:29 and I Corinthians 6:16-17.

21. Kris Lundgaard, *Through the Looking Glass: Reflections on Christ that Change Us* (Phillipsburg, NJ: P&R Publishing Company, 2000), p. 114.

In vain the firstborn seraph tries
to sound the depths of love divine.
'Tis mercy all! Let earth adore;
let angel minds inquire no more[22].

Fourth, we know, from both the Bible and our own consciences, that our sexuality is different than any other bodily appetite. It is much more closely guarded than, say, eating or sleeping is. When it comes to eating, the Bible leaves us free to eat a variety of foods in a variety of ways, but when it comes to having sex, the Bible does not leave us with a lot of choice: it can only be with those of the opposite sex and only if we are in marriage to them and marriage should be with one person and last a lifetime. That's a pretty narrow arena for the satisfying of this basic urge, far more narrow than any other bodily appetite. Then, also, the consequences the Bible gives for sexual sins are greater than the consequences for gluttony or laziness. In fact, we are told that 'Every sin that a man does is outside the body, but he who commits sexual immorality sins against his own body.' (1 Cor. 6:18)

Our consciences also bear witness that there is something unique about our sexuality. We feel no embarrassment at eating openly in front of people. We can usually sleep while others are watching. But seldom is anyone comfortable having sex in front of other people. It's not natural. It's hardwired into us that sex is private and special. Across cultural barriers, people feel greater shame at being raped than at other crimes against them. People think worse of a rapist than of most other criminals. We know instinctively that our sexuality is one of the most precious things we have.

For all these reasons we see that our sexuality is not just one bodily function, one sensual desire, among many, it is special and unique, it is in a class to itself. The more beautiful and valuable something is, the more tragic it is when it is corrupted. When

22. From the hymn 'And Can It Be' by Charles Wesley.

the Fall corrupted our sexuality, it was not the breaking of a soda bottle, it was the breaking of a Tiffany chandelier. This fact almost certainly has something to do with why Adam and Eve were anxious to cover their sexual organs. Sexuality isn't, as some in church history have mistakenly believed, inherently shameful, on the contrary, it is especially beautiful and precious and it is that preciousness which makes it especially shameful when it is corrupted by sin. Whether this is the exact reason why Adam and Eve put on loincloths instead of veils is difficult to know for sure, but we can at least see that our sexuality is precious and that it is closely related to our need for modesty.

C. A Tunic or a Loincloth?

Some reading these things may reach the conclusion that as long as one's sexual organs are covered, one is dressed modestly. If our modesty is all about sexuality, why should we bother to cover any parts of our body not used in intercourse? Why should a woman even cover her breasts? We will look at some other reasons later, but for now while we're looking at Genesis 3, let's see what it has to tell us about this question.

Adam and Eve made for themselves loincloths out of fig leaves, but it is obvious this was not acceptable with God. The main reason it was not acceptable was that it was something of their own making. God was teaching Adam and Eve that they could not make themselves holy. By providing them with clothes of skin, He was teaching them (and us) to look to Him for their righteousness. Many also believe that the fact that animals had to be killed to provide this covering is a picture of how Christ would have to be killed to provide a covering for His people. '…Without shedding of blood there is no remission [for sin]' Hebrews 9:22 teaches us. There was blood shed to provide Adam and Eve with their coverings. For a couple who had never seen death before, what a fearful and terrifying sight that must have been. It surely helped them to see the depths of their Fall. It was not something that could be covered by plucking a few leaves off a tree.

Though that is the primary point this text is making, notice also that God did not make them loincloths of skin. He made them tunics (robes) of skin. It's impossible to know exactly what this looked like as the Hebrew word is a sort of multipurpose word covering several articles of clothing, and that isn't the point anyway. The purpose of God in providing them with robes was not to say that men and women from here on out would have to wear robes, or that they from here on out would have to wear leather or fur, but we can at least recognize that a robe is more substantial than a loincloth, we can at least see an indicator (and later in this book we will look at other evidence as well) that we need to cover more than just our genitals. That this is not just a coincidence is seen in that the vast majority of their descendents have been wearing clothes a great deal more substantial than a loincloth ever since and in that those areas of the world where people do wear loincloths are generally especially degenerate.

Notice also the opposite trade which takes place in Isaiah: Isaiah 3:24 speaks of God judging His people for their unfaithfulness and it says that He will give them 'instead of a rich robe, a girding of sackcloth'[23]. In order to punish them and expose them to the shame they deserved God would strip them of their robes and give them loincloths instead. The idea is that it would be humiliating to go around in nothing more than a loincloth. Although there is no way to tell from Genesis 3

23. The words translated robe and girding are not the same words used in Genesis and the word translated robe is not very clear as to the type of clothing it is referencing. However, in addition to the obvious difference in fabric, clothes made out of sackcloth instead of their previous fine garments, which is part of the humiliation, there is also an evident difference in the coverage offered by the two garments, whatever their exact natures were, the ones they were forced to wear now were comparatively skimpy, and this also is part of the humiliation.

how much of our body must be covered in order to be modest, we can at least recognize that we need to cover substantially more than just our sexual organs. Indeed, when we think that whatever modesty means, it at least means that we need to wear clothes and when we think how little it takes to cover genitalia, especially for a woman, and that such a narrow strip of cloth could hardly be called clothing, then we have further evidence that sexual organs are not the only non-negotiable of modesty.

Maybe some will think this is stating the obvious and I am glad that this much is still obvious in our day. But I am afraid we are approaching a time where these things may not be obvious even among Christians. Can you imagine Christians frequenting topless beaches or Christian women going topless themselves? Christians from 100 years ago couldn't have imagined the bathing suits that many Christian women wear today. Perhaps previous generations of Christians never spelled out the reasons for covering certain parts of the body because it was obvious to everyone and didn't need to be said. Sometimes the obvious needs to be said and defended in order to protect it from being lost by future generations.

3: Defining Modesty

I once worked in the audiovisual department at a large seminary where one of my responsibilities was to be keeper of the keys. I must have had several hundred keys that went to everything from sound booths to media cabinets to padlocks for our data projectors. One day a call came into our office looking for the keys to the piano in the chapel. The call was naturally directed to me and I went looking through all my keys trying to find one that would unlock the piano. I couldn't find anything labeled for the piano so I called down to the music department to see if they had them or knew where they were kept. The first person didn't know anything about keys to the piano, they weren't aware that you could even lock the piano. After a few more calls I finally got someone who knew about the keys. The missing keys, it turned out, were the ones made out of ivory. Never had I imagined that piano keys could be taken out of a piano, but they can, at least in some pianos, and these piano keys had been sent for repairs while the rest of the piano sat in the chapel looking like any other piano until you lifted the lid. We were all speaking English, we were all using the same word, but we were on completely different, dare I say it, octaves. If such misunderstandings can happen with a word as concrete and simple as key, it can certainly happen with a word as intangible and complex as modesty, so we're going to take some time to examine what the word modesty means.

Webster's Dictionary[1] defines 'modest', in part, as 'Observing conventional proprieties in behavior, speech, and dress.' The word 'propriety' is defined as 'Conforming to accepted standards of social conduct.' If this was all that modesty means, this book would not need to be written for the church today is doing a wonderful job of conforming to accepted standards of social conduct! In the pages that follow I will be making the argument that modesty is tied to something more absolute than societal norms, that it is not something that can change by getting on an airplane and going from one part of the world to another, not something that could change by getting in a time machine and going back or forward in time. It will be making the argument that modesty is not about looking around at the behavior, speech, and dress of those around us and falling in line; modesty is about having our minds and hearts renewed by God's Word and from that vantage point seeing how our behavior, speech, and dress should line up with the people He has made us to be.

I am speaking, as I often will be in this book, of modesty in an objective sense: those things that are true of modesty whether we feel them or not. Regardless of whether we feel immodest, it is immodest to walk around in public naked, because it is objectively true that public nudity is immodest. There is also a subjective feeling of modesty, which may or may not line up with what is objectively true. In some cultures, women may feel immodest to show their faces in public, but it is not objectively immodest to do so. Perhaps the biggest threat to modesty today is that it is often thought of as purely subjective – unmoored to anything concrete and free to ride

1. *Riverside Webster's II Dictionary, Revised Edition, 1996.*

the waves of popular opinion with few seeming to notice when she is dashed to pieces on the granite reefs of sensuality.

However, as I seek to show that modesty is objective and unchanging, I would not imply that we can completely disregard the subjective side of modesty, trampling on the feelings people have about decency. If we take an airplane to a part of the world where women wear headscarves, we should take care not to offend their sense of modesty, even though it is not rooted in objective reality. If that is an act of kindness we should be willing to do for complete strangers in cultures where God is blasphemed, how much more should we be willing to show such kindness among those people and in those places where God is worshipped? In these cases it is not as much about modesty as it is about showing that love which honors others above ourselves (Rom. 12:10). There is no harm in covering more of our body than modesty requires and at times it may be the kindest, most considerate thing we can do.

In this chapter we will delve deeper into the meaning of modesty by taking a better look at its English meaning and, more crucial to understanding what the Bible means by modesty, by looking at the Greek words in the classic text on modesty, 1 Timothy 2:9-10.

A. A Little English

Let's start our excursion into the meaning of modesty by looking at the history of the word:

> 'Etymologically linked to the Latin modestus, "keeping within measure", this term originally signified moderation, as in Cicero's "golden mean of living". Gradually, modesty took on the gendered connotation of a sexual virtue particularly important for women.'[2]

---

2. Colin Blakemore and Sheila Jennett. 'modesty.' *The Oxford Companion to the Body*. 2001. Encyclopedia.com. (accessed: June 6, 2015). http://www.encyclopedia.com/doc/1O128-modesty.html.

Another source gives a little more detail, including dates: '1560s, "having moderate self-regard," from Fr. *modeste*, from L. *modestus* "keeping due measure". Of women, "not improper or lewd," 1590s; of female attire, 1610s. Of demands, etc., c.1600.'[3]

So the word modesty started off 500 years ago meaning moderate, measured, the opposite of extreme, extravagant. Within a few decades it was being applied to women who were not lewd and later still to female dress that was not lewd. We don't know for sure why the word took on this sense, but perhaps the idea was of a woman avoiding the extremes both of sexual prudery and of sexual exhibitionism and who was thus moderate in her use of her sexuality. A modest woman [or man], then, is one who is neither shy of sexual matters in an appropriate context nor bold concerning sexual matters in an inappropriate context. Such a person wears clothes in public which are moderate, measured, not extreme or extravagant, clothes which do not flaunt their body.

Today modesty is a word with a broad meaning as well as many nuances and specific usages.[4] This book will be dealing primarily with one very specific and narrow application of modesty: dressing in a way that does not draw sexual attention to one's body. However, it is important to first set this concept in its broader context. Most dictionaries will give several different meanings to the word modest, each with its own specific nuance

---

3. un modest. Dictionary.com. *Online Etymology Dictionary*, Douglas Harper, Historian. (accessed: January 7, 2011). http://dictionary.reference.com/browse/un modest.

4. Dannah Gresh notes that 'Contemporary American culture, by our language, tends to limit modesty to dress. We have one word for modesty and expect it to bear the weight of both the visual modesty as well as the type we can't see. Other languages, including contemporary French, use at least two words to speak of both sexual, physical modesty and that of inner modesty. The Greek culture had *four* words for modesty to differentiate between that which was external and that which was internal.' –*Secret Keeper: The Delicate Power of Modesty* (Moody, 2005), pp. 66-67.

but all bound together with the underlying idea of not calling attention to one's self through extremes. I have consulted a number of dictionaries and thesauruses in compiling the following three facets of modesty:

Humility: having a moderate opinion of one's own abilities and achievements, an unwillingness to draw attention to one's abilities and achievements. Happy to stay in the background. Synonyms are humble, unassuming, self-effacing. Antonyms are proud, arrogant, boastful, vain, conceited, putting oneself forward.

Moderation: moderate in size, amount or extent. A lack of grandeur or flamboyance. Reasonable, not extreme. Synonyms are simple, plain, unexceptional, restrained, reasonable, measured. Antonyms are pretentious, ostentatious, excessive, obtrusive, showy.

Reserve: discreet in appearance, manner, and speech, especially in relation to sexual matters, knowing what is proper or decent and complying. To keep private what should be kept private. Synonyms are decorous, retiring, demure, proper, appropriate, fitting, decent. Antonyms are forward, brazen, bold, assertive, coarse. *(The modesty we will be looking at is a subset of this facet.)*

Some dictionaries will also give an additional facet of modesty: being shy, bashful, timid, prudish. But these things go to the opposite extreme; if modesty is about moderation, then it is not about either extreme, it is not about being prudish or vulgar, timid or brash. As our world becomes increasingly sensual, openly flaunting everything sexual, the modest person may begin to look prudish in comparison, but that is a caricature of modesty and not inherent in its meaning.

From our study of the word modesty, we see that not wearing revealing clothing is not the main meaning of modesty, but is one manifestation of a whole attitude and mindset. Why, then, will we be taking such a careful look at the way we dress? It is popular in most books on modesty to focus on the heart and to make clothing almost an afterthought. It sounds so spiritual, so gospel-centered and non-legalistic, to say that modesty is a heart issue and it really isn't about how you dress[5]. But the Bible doesn't say, 'Let your light so shine before men, that they may see your good hearts and glorify your Father in heaven.' It says your good works.[6] Men cannot see our hearts; men can only see our actions which should reveal what is in our hearts. They know the tree by its fruit.[7] We cannot ultimately have a good heart and bad actions or a bad heart and good actions. Both are oxymorons and both obscure Christ's work in us and tarnish the glory our Father in heaven should be receiving. A modest heart should and will display itself in modest dress.

Modest dress is a manifestation, first of all, of *humility*. A proud person seeks to be noticed, delights to be the center of attention, contrives to be the focal point of admiration. A modest person is not greedy for attention for himself but is generous in giving appropriate attention to others and, above all, seeks to have attention turned to Christ. A proud person will flaunt *his*

---

5. As David and Diane Vaughan say so well, '[in response to a woman who comes to church dressed immodestly but excuses it saying that she had no intention or desire to make anyone lust] "Perhaps [that is so]; but what goes on in the mind or heart is not the standard we live by. The Bible is. And here is where legalism and pietism are in secret league: both substitute the human for the divine. The legalist substitutes human traditions; the pietist substitutes human feelings. If the pietist has all the 'right feelings,' then she has done her duty."' – *The Beauty of Modesty: Cultivating Virtue in the Face of a Vulgar Culture* (Nashville, TN: Cumberland House Publishing, 2005), p. 20.

6. Matthew 5:16.

7. Matthew 7:15-20.

wealth, *his* intelligence, *his* beauty, *his* achievements and one way wealth and beauty in particular can be flaunted is by the way a person dresses. In addition, a proud person will wear whatever he wants without caring how it affects other people. If others find it a temptation or a shock, that's their problem. A humble person imitates Christ by putting others before himself, by being willing to deny himself for the good of others.

Modest dress is a manifestation, secondly, of *moderation*. Moderation avoids extremes and finds the safe, middle ground. It's not too little and it's not too much. It's not rags and it's not riches. It's not austere and it's not flamboyant. When we look at I Timothy 2:9-10, we will find that one of the Greek words regarding a woman's dress is also translated moderation. But here's the vital thing to know about moderation: it is not necessarily following the average person around you, that is, taking your cues from your environment and avoiding being either less or more of something than those around you. A moderate drinker is not one who, when everyone else is drinking themselves under the table, does the same. In drinking moderately he will, in such a situation, be noticeable for how much less he drinks than anyone else. Speaking moderately does not mean that if everyone else is ranting and screaming that you rant and scream along with the average of them. You may again stand out because you are the only one speaking moderately. It is the same with dressing modestly in a world where immodesty is rife. You will be noticed.

Many people believe that it is an automatic crime against modesty to stand out, but this is a misunderstanding of what modesty is. If modesty and godliness were all about not drawing attention to ourselves then we would not have been told to be cities set on a hill, lights put on a candlestick.[8] Light draws

8. Matthew 5:14-15.

attention to itself and the darker the surroundings, the more attention it draws. Others will, as I Peter 4:4 puts it, 'think it strange that you do not run with them in the same flood of dissipation' (KJV: to the same excess of riot). The KJV translates Philippians 4:5, 'Let your moderation[9] be known unto all men. The Lord is at hand.'

As the Puritan, Richard Baxter, wrote in his *Christian Directory*, there is a time when singularity in dress is our duty.[10] We should not dress modestly *for the sake of* standing out, but we will at times need to dress modestly *at the price of* standing out. We could put it this way: to dress more modestly than necessary for the sake of drawing attention to oneself is *exhibitionism*; to dress less modestly than necessary for the sake of not drawing attention is *conformity*, to dress as modestly as necessary for the sake of pleasing God is *luminosity*.

Modest dress is lastly, and this is what we will particularly have in view as we go along, a manifestation of *reserve in sexual matters*. It is the opposite of brazenness or vulgarity. A modest person is one who is not forward to talk about sexual things nor show parts of the body that arouse sexual thoughts. It's not necessarily about embarrassment, it's certainly not that these things are bad; it's that they are private things and not meant to be made public. A modest person knows this and is reticent of speaking about them inappropriately; a brazen person will talk about anything, anytime with anyone. A modest person has

---

9. The word 'moderation' here, which the NKJV translates gentleness, is a different Greek word than the one translated moderation in 1 Timothy 2:9.

10. 'Affect not singularity in your apparel; that is, to be odd and observably distinct from all those of your own rank and quality; unless their fashions be evil and intolerable, (in pride, immodesty, levity, &c.) and then your singularity is your duty.' – Richard Baxter, 'Christian Ethics' (ch. 10, part 3, direction 3) in *The Practical Works of Richard Baxter*, p. 391.

a certain reserve in his interactions, especially with those of the opposite sex; a brazen person is careless and enjoys testing the limits, especially with those of the opposite sex. A modest person dresses in public in a way that is not sexualized, does not reveal more of his body than would be edifying to those around him; a brazen person goes around in public dressed in ways which incite lust and enjoys the feeling that others are staring.

There is a lovely description of this aspect of modesty in Song of Solomon 4:12:

> 'A garden enclosed
> Is my sister, my spouse,
> A spring shut up,
> A fountain sealed.'

The language of garden, spring and fountain is used to image sexuality[11]. Now notice the words enclosed, shut up, sealed. These are words of reserve, of modesty. Modesty is not the repression of something repugnant, but the guarding, the treasuring of something beautiful.

B. A LITTLE GREEK: I TIMOTHY 2:8-10

The Bible doesn't say a lot directly on the subject of modesty, but we're going to take a close look at what it does say and to do that we're going to have to learn a little Greek. It's not enough just to know what the dictionary definition is; we need to know what the Bible means by modesty. And we may be in for a bit of a surprise, for the words in the 'proof text' on modesty don't all mean what they seem to mean:

> 1 Timothy 2:8-10, 'I desire therefore that the men pray everywhere, lifting up holy hands, without wrath and doubting;

11. See Proverbs 5:15-19 and Song of Solomon 4:1-5:1 for examples of this imagery.

> in like manner also, that the women adorn themselves in **modest** apparel, with **propriety** and **moderation**[12], not with braided hair or gold or pearls or costly clothing, but, which is proper for women professing godliness, with good works.'

Kosmios

Kosmios is the word translated modest; it is only used twice in the Bible and *Strong's Concordance* defines it as 'orderly, decorous [e.g. proper].' The ESV translates this word as 'respectable'.

To get a better picture of this word, we need to look at its roots. *Kosmios* is the adjective form of the word *kosmos* which is most often translated 'world' and from which we get the English words cosmos and cosmetics. *Kosmos,* at its most basic, *Vine's Dictionary* tells us, means 'a harmonious arrangement or order.' Out of that definition came the meaning 'adornment, decoration' and from there it came to mean 'the world, or the universe, as that which is divinely arranged.' It is not surprising that our world, being exactly the right distance from the sun, having exactly the right composition in the air for life, keeping everything in perfect balance, should become synonymous with the word order. Not only this, but God made the world more than merely functional, He made it beautiful. It is adorned to give pleasure to the eye. *Kosmos* captures both its orderliness and its beauty.

Kosmos is the word used in the companion verse to 1 Timothy 2:9, I Peter 3:3, where it is translated 'adornment': 'Do not let your **adornment** be merely outward – arranging the hair, wearing gold, or putting on fine apparel.' In 1 Timothy 2:9 the verb form of *Kosmos*, as well as the adjective form, is used : 'In like manner also, that the women **adorn** [*Kosmeo*] themselves in **modest** [*Kosmios*] apparel, with propriety and moderation…'

---

12. Any time words in Scripture are in bold, it is my (the author's) emphasis.

The second and last time the adjective form *Kosmios* is used is a few verses later in regard to pastors where it is translated 'of good behavior': 'A bishop then must be blameless, the husband of one wife, temperate, sober-minded, of **good behavior** [*Kosmios*], hospitable, able to teach; (in NKJV)' 1 Timothy 3:2. (The ESV translates *Kosmios* here as respectable, as it did in 1 Timothy 2:9.) Here the word is being used to describe, not clothing, but character. A pastor especially is to live his life in a way that is orderly and decent. As with an orderly world, the resulting impression of such a character will be one of beauty and attractiveness, a character which could be said to 'adorn [*Kosmeo*] the doctrine of God,' as is said of the obedience and faithfulness of servants in Titus 2:10.

So whether it is the earth, our behavior or our clothes, the underlying theme of *Kosmos* and its derivatives is of being arranged orderly and adorned ornamentally. *Kosmios* has the added emphasis on being fitting or proper. In the excellent booklet *Dressed to Kill*, it says regarding this passage, 'Kenneth Wuest, the longtime Greek professor at Moody Bible Institute, explains the word's meaning in this particular passage: it speaks of an orderly and appropriate relationship between one's clothing and one's Christian character.'[13] Let's now look at those qualities of our Christian character our clothing should, according to this passage, especially be in keeping with: propriety and moderation.

Aidos

Aidos is the word translated 'propriety' in I Timothy 2:8-10[14] in the NKJV. The ESV translates it 'modesty.' *Strong's* describes it as

13. Robert G. Spinney, *Dressed to Kill: Thinking Biblically About Modest and Immodest Clothing* (Hartsville, TN: Tulip Books, 2007), p. 5.

14. *Aidos* is only used one other time and that is in Hebrews 12:28 (although some manuscripts instead use *deos* meaning awe) where it speaks of serving God acceptably with reverence.

'bashfulness', and says that in regards to people this bashfulness can be thought of as modesty and in regards to God it can be thought of as awe. *Strong's* also says that the word is derived from a combination of two other words through the idea of 'downcast eyes.'

Vine's quotes Trench as describing it, in part, as 'an innate moral repugnance to the doing of the dishonorable act.'

The KJV translates this word as shamefacedness and a couple of commentaries further explain this idea:

> 'Shamefacedness' is really 'shamefastness'-standing fast in modesty, not bold or self-assertive, nor flaunting personal charms...[15] *Addresses on the First and Second Epistles of Timothy* by H. A. Ironside.

> It is 'what is made fast, and "held fast, by an honourable shame".'[16] *Practical Truths from the Pastoral Epistles* by Eugene Stock.

Aidos, then, is feeling shame at what is shameful and being deterred by that shame from doing it. *Aidos* is unassuming, it does not seek attention and it especially does not seek wrong attention. It is this word that brings in the reserve aspect of modesty into this passage.

Sophrosune

This is the word the NKJV translates as 'moderation'. Strong's gives the synonyms of sobriety, soundness of mind, sanity, self-control, soberness, reason. The ESV translates it 'self-control'. This word is used in Acts 26:25 when Paul tells Festus, 'I am not mad, but speak the words of truth and *reason*' and in 1 Timothy 2:15 when women are told they will be saved in childbearing if they 'continue in faith, love, and holiness, with *self-control*.'

---

15. H. A. Ironside, *Addresses on the First and Second Epistles of Timothy* (Loizeaux Brothers), p. 63.
16. Eugene Stock, *Practical Truths from the Pastoral Epistles* (Grand Rapids, MI: Kregel Publications, 1983), p. 204.

Sophrosune comes from the word *sophron* which is a compound of *soos* (safe or sound) and *phren* (mind). The most literal translation, then, is sound mind. *Strong's* describes *sophron* as discreet, temperate, sober, moderate as to opinion or passion. In I Timothy 3:2 and Titus 1:8 *sophron* is listed as one of the qualifications for being a pastor. In Titus 2:2 older men are told they should be 'sober, reverent, *temperate* [*sophron*], sound in faith, in love, in patience' and a few verses later young women are admonished to be '*discreet* [*sophron*].'

The commentator Eugene Stock writes of *sophrosune*, 'The Greeks generally used the word to express self-restraint, and in Aristotle it signifies mastery over bodily passions.... There are no English words that exactly translate [this word]....' He goes on to quote Ellicott as calling it 'sober-mindedness,' and describing it as 'the well-balanced state of mind arising from habitual self-restraint."[17] It carries the meaning of thinking through something carefully and using good judgment. [18]

If all we had to do to be modest was to follow what others around us were doing, it would not take much sober judgment. Nothing is easier than doing what others around us are doing. If the Bible had given a specific set of standards for modesty and all we had to do was follow those standards, again it would not take much sober judgment. Few things are easier than following a list of rules. As David and Diane Vaughan put it, '... learning

17. Stock, *Practical Truths from the Pastoral Epistles*, pp. 267-268.

18. It also has been said of sophrosune that, 'It signifies entire command of the passions and desires; a self-control which holds the rein over these.' –Marvin R. Vincent in *Word Studies in the New Testament, Volume III* (Grand Rapids, MI: WM. B Eerdmans, 1989).

specifics requires only knowledge, whereas learning and applying principles requires wisdom and maturity…'[19] When it comes to modesty, we are told, not to find easy answers, but to exercise *sophrosune*.

Later we will come back to this verse and unpack more of its meaning, but for now let's put together what we have learned from these three Greek words. From the word *kosmios* we learned that our clothes should be orderly and proper. Part of that means that our clothes should be in keeping with our Christian character. We should not be one thing on the inside and appear to be something else on the outside. A modest heart should choose to wear modest clothes. That is only fitting and proper. The word orderly also implies thought, planning and preparation. We can't just throw something on without thinking about it. When God created the world, He didn't just throw a bunch of stuff together to see what would happen. He had a plan, He took thought and He designed a world that is both functional and beautiful.

The word *sophrosune* reinforces this idea. It teaches us that we are to dress in a way that shows sobriety, soundness of mind, good judgment. One of the reasons women do not understand what draws wrong attention to themselves is that they don't take modesty seriously. The more sober-minded women are, the better judgments they will make. However, young women especially are known for being emotional, spontaneous, naïve, even silly. When it comes to clothes, they love to go shopping with their friends for fun, trying on clothes and exclaiming about how cute something is. Serious thought isn't usually on the agenda. I Timothy 2 is telling us that it needs to be put on the agenda. What we wear is serious and we need to treat it as

---

19. David Vaughan and Diane Vaughan, *The Beauty of Modesty*, p. 21.

such. This doesn't mean shopping can't be fun, that clothes can't be cute, it means that it can't all be fun and games, it can't all be about what is cute. We need to practice that 'habitual self-restraint', which will give rise to a 'well-balanced state of mind.'

As we think carefully about what we wear, one trait that should frame our thinking is captured by *aidos*, that quality which causes a person to feel shame at things that are shameful. Such a woman realizes that certain parts of her body are meant to be private and she would be ashamed to have those parts put on public display. It is not shame about her body or shame about her sexuality; it is shame about the wrong use of her body and her sexuality that motivates her modesty. A modest woman may eagerly welcome her husband to visually consume her body, but to have a stranger ogle her is disturbing, even revolting and so she is careful to choose clothes that do not prompt that.

The second chapter in the book of 1 Timothy does not have anything to say about our hemlines or our necklines. There is no way to study the Greek to find out how long our skirts should be or how high our tops should be. But the more we cultivate the attitudes and thinking that this passage highlights, the more our understanding will be enlightened and the better we can discern what we should wear. In other words, the more our windshield will be defrosted and the better we'll be able to see where the ditch is and where the centerline is and stay between the two.

One thing you may have noticed, both in the etymology of the English word and in the Bible's exhortation on modesty, is that modesty is especially important for women. This fact is not popular in our day, it seems sexist and chauvinistic, but it is undeniable that the Bible singles women out for instruction on modesty. This indicates that it is especially important for women to be modest and that women especially are tempted to be immodest. This is certainly not to say that it's okay for men to be immodest but there are a number of virtues which, while they are good for everyone to have, are especially important for a particular gender to have. Both men and women should be brave, but cowardice is worse in a man than in a woman. Both men and women should be gentle, but harshness is worse in a woman than in a man. Modesty, especially in the sense of sexual reserve, is, particularly, though not exclusively, a female virtue (something even psychologists have recognized[20]). There is a reason we speak of blushing brides and not blushing grooms.

C. A Little More Greek: I Corinthians 12:23-24

There is one more place where the Bible speaks directly on modesty:

> 'And those members of the body which we think to be less honorable, on these we bestow greater honor; and our unpresentable parts have greater **modesty**, but our presentable parts have no need. But God composed the body, having given greater honor to that part which lacks it'. (1 Cor. 12:23-24)

Euschemosune and its relatives

The word translated modesty is *euschemosune*. *Thayer's Bible Dictionary* describes it as external beauty, decorum, modesty, seemliness, comeliness. This is the only time this particular word is used in the Bible, but it is derived from the word ***euschemona*, which can mean either proper, sometimes in the sense of sexually proper[21], or honorable. *Euschmona* is also**

20. 'Modesty,...while common to both sexes is more peculiarly feminine, so that it may almost be regarded as the chief secondary sexual character of women on the psychical side.' – Havelock Ellis, *Studies in the Psychology of Sex, Volume 1* (F.A. Davis Company, 1910), p. 1.
21. It is used in the sense of sexually proper in Paul's advice to single men

used in this passage: 'our **presentable parts** (***euschemona***) have no need [of covering or modesty].' Both of these words (*euschemosune* and *euschemona*) are the combination of *eu* (good) and *schema* (shape, form, appearance).

The opposite word, *aschemon* (*a* (without) + *schema*), is also used in this passage: 'and our **unpresentable parts** (*aschemon*) have [as in, they require] greater modesty.' This word means unseemly, indecent. This is the only time the word is used in the New Testament, but it is used twice in the Septuagint (the Greek translation of the Old Testament widely used in Jesus' day) where it has the meaning of sexually improper[22]. This is also the meaning when the verb form of *aschemon* is used in I Corinthians 7:36: 'But if any man thinks he is **behaving improperly** (*aschemoneo*) toward his virgin...' A derivative of this word is used in Romans 1:27 where it again has a sexual connotation: 'Likewise also the men, leaving the natural use of the woman, burned in their lust for one another, men with men committing what is **shameful** (*aschemosune*), and receiving in themselves the penalty of their error which was due.'

Calling these parts unpresentable does not mean they are ugly or bad, for many of these same parts are described with

---

in I Corinthians 7:35, 'And this I say for your own profit, not that I may put a leash on you, but for what is proper (***euschemona***), and that you may serve the Lord without distraction.' The adverb form is used in the same sense in Romans 13:13, 'Let us walk properly (*euschemonos*), as in the day, not in revelry and drunkenness, not in lewdness and lust, not in strife and envy.'

22. Genesis 34:7, 'And the sons of Jacob came in from the field when they heard it; and the men were grieved and very angry, because he had done a **disgraceful** thing in Israel by lying with Jacob's daughter, a thing which ought not to be done.' Deuteronomy 24:1, 'When a man takes a wife and marries her, and it happens that she finds no favor in his eyes because he has found some **uncleanness** in her...'

much rapture and delight in Song of Solomon. Though they are shameful to be exposed publicly, they are some of the greatest charms in the marriage bed.

From these things we can make four observations:

1. There are parts of our body that need covering in public (unpresentable parts) and parts of our body that do not need covering (presentable parts).

2. In covering our unpresentable parts, we honor our body. We don't do it because we hate these parts or think they are ugly, but because we value them and want to honor them. This is important because many who dress immodestly say they do it because they love their bodies and aren't ashamed of them. The Bible teaches us something very different, it teaches us that a high regard for our bodies will cause us to cover those parts which decency requires.

3. The arguments given for modesty are not about honoring one's culture, but honoring one's body. In this we see that the need for modesty is not something hoisted on us by our culture, but something innate to our humanity. The problem with immodesty, then, is not that it offends one's culture, but that it shames one's own body.

4. Though we are not told which parts are presentable and which are not, there is an indication of what makes them presentable or unpresentable. When we look at the way *aschemon* and its derivatives are used elsewhere, they most often have the meaning, not of socially proper, but of sexually proper. Modesty, then, is about honoring the sexuality of our bodies. Again we see evidence (and we will look at more in a later chapter) that modesty is not a societal construct.

As John MacArthur wrote in his Bible study on this section, 'It is a normal, human reaction to cover the private or indecent parts of the human body, not just for the sake of adornment, but for the sake of modesty, with even a greater amount of effort. To show you how far away we have gone from what is normally human, just look at our society today. Those parts of the human body which mankind has long known to be private, and which ought to be covered with honor so that they can be held in modesty, are now exploited. That just shows how far our depravity has gone.'[23]

If all of this sounds legalistic and you think we should just focus on love, let me share with you what the Bible says about love, where it just so happens that our word is found again: '[Love] doth not behave itself unseemly *(aschemoneo)*' (1 Cor. 13:5, KJV). This is the same chapter that tells us that love is the greatest thing, but it does not leave us to define and live out love however we want, it tells us what love is and what it isn't, what it does and what it doesn't do. A list of do's and don'ts, if you will! And one of the don'ts of love is that it does not behave itself in a sexually improper way, including showing publically our 'unpresentable' parts. You may speak with the tongues of men and of angels, you may give all of your goods to feed the poor, you may even give your life as a martyr, but if you do not have love in all of its aspects, including behaving in a way that is seemly and decent, it will all amount to nothing.[24]

D. DEFINITIONS FROM OTHERS

As we saw earlier, modesty, as it relates to clothes, has two main elements: one that is more sexually orientated and is

23. John MacArthur, Jr, *Spiritual Gifts* [originally titled *The Power of Jesus*] (Chicago: Moody Press, 1983), p. 260.

24. Besides the places already referenced, *aschemon* and its derivatives are used in only one other place and that is in Revelation 16:15, 'Blessed is he who watches, and keeps his garments, lest he walk naked and they see his shame *(aschemosune)*.'

about what parts of the body you expose, and one that is more materialistically orientated and is about the extravagance of the clothes you wear. The common element is drawing wrong attention to yourself, either encouraging others to lust after your body or else encouraging others to envy your wealth. Both forms of immodesty can be a problem, but this book will deal mainly with modesty as it relates to exposing our body because it is arguably the bigger problem in today's world and because it is the less understood problem.

The fashion historian James Laver, hardly a friend to modesty, gives a definition of this facet of modesty that is not bad: 'The modest woman is one who does not exploit any of the available devices for drawing attention to her sexual attractions.'[25]

The Puritan Vincent Alsop wrote, 'Modesty teaches us not to expose those parts to view that no necessity, no good end or use will justify.'[26]

Pastor Greg Nichols in a series on Christian Modesty gives a thorough and well-rounded definition of modesty: 'reluctance to draw undue attention to yourself; reserve about public nudity, commitment to wear clothes in public that cover the body decently and sensibly; moderation; a lack of ostentation.'[27]

Pastor Jeff Pollard gives a definition that captures the heart of it: 'Christian modesty is the inner self-government, rooted in a proper understanding of one's self before God, which outwardly displays itself in humility and purity from a genuine

---

25. James Laver, *Modesty in Dress: An Inquiry into the Fundamentals of Fashion* (Houghton Mifflin Company, 1969), p. 9.

26. Vincent Alsop, 'What Distance Ought We to Keep, in Following the Strange Fashions of Apparel Which Come Up in the Days Wherein We Live?' in *Puritan Sermons 1659-1689* (Richard Owen Roberts, Publishers) quoted in *Free Grace Broadcaster* no. 216 (Summer 2011): pp. 23-24.

27. Gregory G. Nichols, *Christian modesty* (sermon series on Sermon Audio, April-June 2010). http://www.sermonaudio.com/sermoninfo.asp?SID=427101543479

love for Jesus Christ, rather than in self-glorification or self-advertisement.'[28]

The sexologist Havelock Ellis wrongly believed that modesty is partly a fear of causing desire and partly a fear of causing disgust.[29] In other words, people wear clothes either because they are nervous about sex and afraid of receiving sexual attention or because they are self-conscious about their body and afraid of being held in contempt. That this is often what causes people to cover their bodies, is true enough, but that this should be the basis for modesty, is absolutely false. Biblical modesty is not rooted in fear, it is not rooted in trepidation toward things sexual and it is not rooted in doubts about the acceptability of our bodies. It is this misunderstanding that makes people believe that a healthy body image and a healthy view of sex will keep people from being 'puritanical' about modesty. One of the purposes of this book is to show that the very opposite is the case: a biblical body image and a biblical view of sex are the greatest and best motivations for Christian modesty.

Earlier we saw that modesty is a feeling of shame at what is shameful. Ellis, however, is speaking of a misplaced shame, a shame of our bodies. There is nothing to be embarrassed about our bodies, our bodies are beautiful; it is the public display of nakedness that is shameful. This is an important distinction to keep in mind because this book will quote people who use shame in both these senses, so in one place we will be saying that modesty is about shame and in other places we will be saying that modesty is not about shame. Modesty is about moderation, being ashamed of what is shameful, but not ashamed of what

---

28. Jeff Pollard, *Christian Modesty and the Public Undressing of America* (Pensacola, FL: Mt Zion Publications), p. 7.

29. Havelock Ellis, *Studies in the Psychology of Sex, Volume 1* (F.A. Davis Company, 1910), pp. 48-49.

is not shameful. We are not, for instance, to be ashamed of the gospel of God for there is certainly nothing in the least shameful about it.

My favorite description is probably the one by James Spiegel in *How to be Good in a World Gone Bad*, which so perfectly refutes Ellis' definition:

> 'Modesty is *not* bashfulness [author: that is, it is not a fear of causing desire]. The modest person freely chooses to keep certain things private and he does so out of respect for others as well as himself. The shy person's timidity, on the other hand, is not a choice. He keeps things private inadvertently, out of fear. So his real concern is not others but himself. Whereas the bashful person finds revealing himself in public uncomfortable, the modest person keeps a thing out of public view for the sake of others, even if he would personally be comfortable revealing more.
>
> 'Modesty is *not* shame [author: that is, it is not a fear of causing disgust].... Modesty is motivated by self-respect and appreciation for one's own body, and it's because of this bodily self-respect that the modest individual keeps it private.'[30]

Or, in the words of Wendy Shalit,

> 'Modesty is not about shame...it derives from knowing the true worth of something.'[31]

This is too important to pass over quickly. It is not enough to dress modestly, women in the Taliban dress more modestly than almost anyone, women who hate their bodies also tend to cover them up as much as possible. In order to please God, which is

30. Spiegel, *How to Be Good*, p. 139.

31. Wendy Shalit, *Girls Gone MILD: Young Women Reclaim Self-Respect and Find It's Not Bad to Be Good* (New York: Random House, 2007), p. 162.

our goal as Christians, we must dress modestly for the right reasons, so let's take a closer look at how we should think of our bodies and our beauty. The next two chapters will be speaking particularly to women, but men need to hear these things too, both for their own sakes and for the sake of passing these truths on to the women under their care.

4: Modesty, Beauty and the Human Body

Modesty is not about covering up your body because you think it is ugly, modesty is realizing that God made the human body, *your* body, beautiful and that its beauty is something personal and meant to be enjoyed in intimate settings.

A. Modesty believes that the human body is beautiful

Fundamental to true Christian modesty is the belief that our bodies are incredibly good, incredibly beautiful. C.S. Lewis says that 'Christianity is almost the only one of the great religions which thoroughly approves of the body – which believes that matter is good, that God Himself once took on a human body, that some kind of body is going to be given to us even in Heaven and is going to be an essential part of our happiness, our beauty and our energy.'[1]

1. C.S. Lewis, *Mere Christianity* (New York: HarperCollins Publishers, 2001), p. 98.

However, it is possible there has never been a time when so few women believed that their bodies are beautiful and this may explain the scandalously increasing immodesty of our time. This is true even of Christians because we pay so much attention to what the world says and so little attention to what God says.

Let's look at what God says. When God saw everything He had made, He said it was good (Gen. 1:31). One of the things He had made was the human body – and as yet there were no clothes on those bodies. The human body (and especially a woman's body) is one of the most beautiful sights there is and an appreciation for the beauty of a body is a pleasure that has been given to us by our good God, a pleasure designed to be enjoyed in its fullest in marriage. This is illustrated almost shockingly in the book of Song of Solomon:

> How beautiful are your feet in sandals,
> O prince's daughter!
> The curves of your thighs are like jewels,
> The work of the hands of a skillful workman.
> Your navel is a rounded goblet;
> It lacks no blended beverage.
> Your waist is a heap of wheat
> Set about with lilies.
> Your two breasts are like two fawns,
> Twins of a gazelle.
> Your neck is like an ivory tower,
> Your eyes like the pools in Heshbon
> By the gate of Bath Rabbim.
> Your nose is like the tower of Lebanon
> Which looks toward Damascus.
> Your head crowns you like Mount Carmel,
> And the hair of your head is like purple;
> A king is held captive by your tresses.
> How fair and how pleasant you are,

> O love, with your delights!
> This stature of yours is like a palm tree,
> And your breasts like its clusters.
> I said, 'I will go up to the palm tree,
> I will take hold of its branches.'
> Let now your breasts be like clusters of the vine,
> The fragrance of your breath like apples,
> And the roof of your mouth like the best wine.
> The wine goes down smoothly for my beloved,
> Moving gently the lips of sleepers. (Song 7:1-9)

It is true that after the Fall, sin entered the world and things are not perfect anymore. Even so, God's creation still bears the fingerprints of the God who created it, a God who delights in beauty. Nature may not be perfect anymore, but it is still often stunningly beautiful as a trip to the Grand Canyon or the Alps will prove. Likewise, even though no one's body is perfect, the human body still shows God's craftsmanship and has a wondrous beauty of its own. In 1 Corinthians 15:40 it says, 'There are also celestial bodies and terrestrial bodies; but the glory of the celestial is one and the glory of the terrestrial is another.' Terrestrial, earthly bodies have a glory, a dignity, a beauty. True, it is not the same glory that our new bodies will have when we get to heaven, but they are still wonderfully and marvelously made.

This may be easy to believe when it comes to the human body in general, but what about when it comes to your body? Do you believe that your body shows God's craftsmanship and has a wondrous beauty of its own? It is true whether you believe it or not, but believing it is foundational to truly being modest.

The biggest reason it is so hard for women to believe that their bodies are beautiful is because they are too busy listening to the lies of the world. The world is constantly feeding us images of women who look more like Barbie dolls than real women and telling us that is what it means to be beautiful. Carolyn Mahaney describes today's situation well:

> In previous centuries, women might have compared themselves with the other 10 women in the village; today women compare themselves with pictures of the supermodels put on display by the worldwide fashion industry. That image of beauty is so narrow in its range that most women feel unattractive in comparison.
>
> Even worse is the deception in the fashion industry itself. Did you know that most of the models we see in the magazines don't even look like their own pictures? Fashion magazine editors admit that almost every photograph of a model has been digitally altered. So think about it: This alluring model has been toned by her personal trainer, had her hair done by a professional stylist, her face painted by a professional makeup artist, and her image captured by a professional photographer under ideal lightning. After this, if the model *still* doesn't look good enough, she is recast through computer graphics.[2]

But there is a deception even more basic than these things found in our very idea of beauty. Have you ever stopped to think about why we find some physical characteristics beautiful and others ugly? Why do people want a tan? Why do people of a healthy weight want to be thinner? Are these universal standards of beauty that people everywhere have sought after? As we will soon see, no, they are not. Valerie Steele writes, 'To a considerable extent, beauty is not even a physical given, but an artificial construct that varies from culture to culture.'[3] This is not what beauty should be, but this is how beauty is popularly conceived.

---

2. Carolyn Mahaney, 'True Beauty' in *Biblical Womanhood in the Home* ed. Nancy Leigh DeMoss (Wheaton, IL: Crossway Books, 2002), p. 35.

3 Valerie Steele, *Fashion and Eroticism: Ideals of Feminine Beauty from the Victorian Era to the Jazz Age* (New York: Oxford University Press, 1985), p. 41.

There is a general principle that whatever is difficult for the average person to obtain is likely to be considered beautiful. It is not the intrinsic value of a feature, but the time, money and effort required, that matters. Consider food for a moment. It is not that caviar tastes better than apples that gives it its prestige, but the fact that caviar is an indication of wealth while anyone can afford an apple. In the same way that caviar is more of a status symbol than something truly tasty, so some features considered beautiful are more of a status symbol than something truly beautiful.

In some places ridiculously long fingernails – to us they look more like claws – have been thought beautiful. Since they showed that the wearer didn't have to engage in manual labor, they suggested prosperity and refinement. One Chinese princess had intricately carved nail protectors to wear over her 6 inch long fingernails.[4] In places in Africa it used to be a mark of beauty to have one's teeth filed to a point. For many years in China small feet, extremely small with the ideal being 2 inches, were considered beautiful. One observer wrote that 'the butler's little daughter, aged seven, is having her feet "bandaged" for the first time, and is in torture, but bears it bravely in the hope of "getting a rich husband."'[5] For the rest of their lives these girls would walk painfully on misshapen feet – all in the name of beauty.

There are many examples in our own backyard. Take the current premium on tans, for instance.

For many centuries, probably millennia, a tan was a sign of someone who did manual labor, which was usually outdoors, while white skin showed that you didn't have to work and were

4 Jane Bingham, *A History of Fashion and Costume, Volume 1: The Ancient World* (Bailey Publishing Associates, 2005), p. 48.

5 Valerie Steele and John S. Major, *China Chic: East Meets West* (Yale University Press, 1999), p. 42.

more likely to be upper-class. Books often described a heroine's 'lily white' skin. When a lady was outdoors she carried a parasol to shield her face from the sun. As menial labor moved indoors, to factories and offices, white skin became the norm among the lower class. Now a tan implied, not that you worked out in the sun, but that you had money to lie around in the sun or, especially if you were tanned in the winter, to take vacations to the French Riviera or some other warm spot. Heroines in books started being described as having 'bronzed' skin. For a while the darker the tan, the more beautiful, but as the dangers of skin cancer became better known and as tanning beds made tans easier to achieve and thus less prestigious, the ideal color has become a medium tan.[6]

Perhaps the thing that has changed the most often in the history of beauty ideals is whether thin is beautiful or whether large is beautiful. Believe it or not, large has more often won the day. In the late nineteenth century the book *Beauty and How to Keep It* by Professional Beauty (that really is how the author's name is given!) stated, 'Extreme thinness is a much more cruel enemy to beauty than extreme stoutness.'[7] At this time, a beautiful leg was considered to be a round and plump leg.[8] There were creams on the market which promised to make the arm and neck fatter, as much, it was claimed, as 30 pounds fatter.[9] And even 'extreme stoutness' has on occasion been 'in'. In Africa, in what is now Uganda, in the nineteenth century, obese was beautiful. The

---

6. Alison Lurie, *The Language of Clothes* (New York: Random House, 1981), p. 235.
7. A Professional Beauty, *Beauty and How to Keep It*, 47-49, quoted in Valerie Steele, *Fashion and Eroticism: Ideals of Feminine Beauty from the Victorian Era to the Jazz Age* (New York: Oxford University Press, 1985), p. 108.
8. Steele, *Fashion and Eroticism*, p. 222.
9. Ibid., p. 221.

kings wives were fed a beer and honey mixture until they were so fat they couldn't stand on their own two feet.

In our own day and land the desirable body image is youthful, very thin, with large breasts. This is a perfect example of the irrationality of cultural beauty ideals. In nature, thin and large breasts don't usually go together; to achieve this effect usually requires either surgery (one of the most popular cosmetic surgeries, increasingly given to young women as graduation gifts[10]) or a Wonder bra. Real beauty, however, is about proportion and that is how God has designed things: A large woman will usually have large breasts and a slender woman will usually have small breasts.

Robert Musil, an Austrian writer and nominee for the Nobel Prize, describes this state of affairs well in his novel, translated into English as *The Man Without Qualities*, 'There are, of course, in all periods all kinds of countenances, but only one type will be singled out by a period's taste as its ideal image of happiness and beauty while all the other faces do their best to copy it, and with the help of fashion and hairdressers even the ugly ones manage to approximate the ideal. But there are some faces that never succeed, faces born to a strange distinction of their own, unyieldingly expressing the regal and banished ideal beauty of an earlier period.'[11]

If we can't, then, measure up to the current ideal of beauty, we can at least think of ourselves as having 'that regal and banished beauty' of a bygone era!

---

10. See the article by Robin Henig, 'The Price of Perfection' *Civilization* (April 1996). http://www.nasw.org/users/robinhenig/price_of_perfection.htm.

11 Robert Musil, *Mannen uten egenskaper: Volume 1*, (Solum, 2000), p. 20, quoted in Lars Svendsen, *Fashion: A Philosophy* tr. John Irons (London: Reakton Books, 2006), pp. 80-81.

Variety in Beauty

'Fair' the hymn 'Fairest Lord Jesus' says 'are the meadows, fairer still the woodlands, robed in the blooming garb of spring... Fair is the sunshine, fairer still the moonlight, and all the twinkling starry host...Jesus is fairer.....' God is so beautiful and wonderful that He had to create many different types of beauty to try to display it all. Nothing is as beautiful and wonderful as God, but different things show a little piece of His beauty and wonder. Satan hates God, hates anything that reminds him of God. Could it be that he is behind the pitting of one form of beauty against another, brown skin against white skin, large figures against small figures; could he be behind the monstrosities which have been given the misnomer of beauty, everything from six inch long fingernails to two inch long feet, from anorexic girls with breast implants in America to obese women who can't walk without help in Africa?

God has given us the gift of variety, a variety of different ways to be beautiful. We are not living according to truth when we feel ugly because we do not measure up to the world's arbitrary, narrow and ultimately godless definition of beauty. We recognize in nature that there are many forms of beauty, the beauty of the seashore is one, the beauty of the meadows is another, and the beauty of the mountains is still another. What if one day a man decided that the mountains were the only thing beautiful and everything else should try as much as possible to look like mountains? People living by the seashore pay money to bring huge boulders to hide the sea from view, truck in a lot of dirt and plant some grass and trees. People living in the meadows follow his advice to mow down all the flowers, truck in as much dirt and rocks as possible to approximate a mountain and then plant some trees. Let's say this man writes best-selling books on how to landscape your yard to make your home look as much as possible as if it were in the mountains. All he would succeed in doing is robbing the seashore (and the meadows, the forest, the rolling hills, etc.) of their beauty. Now everywhere you look, all you see is strange, ugly mountains. And what about those people who prefer the seashore to the mountains? Who was this man to decide that the mountains and only the mountains were beautiful? He would justly deserve to be considered nothing less than a madman by all those who love nature.

As crazy as this would be, it is just as crazy to deny the beauty of different body types and try to make them all look alike. But this is exactly what the world does. It tells one person that their breasts are too big and sells them a minimizing bra, it tells the next person that their breasts are too small and sells them a maximizing bra. It may at one time sell curling irons to everyone with straight hair and at another time sell flattening irons to everyone with curly hair. It may on one side of the globe sell whitening creams to Asians while on the other side selling tanning creams to Caucasians. Women's magazines are filled with advice on how to buy jeans and bathing suits for whatever figure type you have in order to make it look more like the accepted figure type. It doesn't matter that men have different tastes and not all men like the same body type, the world has decided this or that is beautiful and everyone else needs to fall in line or feel bad about not being able to fall in line.

Let's personalize the seashore for a minute. What would we think if we found Miss Seashore glumly looking through catalogs filled with glossy, full-color, full-page photos of some of the world's most stunning mountains, not a tree out of place, then we watched as Miss Seashore trudged out to the store to buy some rocks and trees which the magazine told her might be able to 'enhance her landscape' all the while knowing it is a lost cause, that try as she might she will never look like those mountains in the magazine? Wouldn't we want her to understand that we think she is beautiful the way she is and that we don't want her to look like the mountains? Wouldn't we tell her that God made her that way and that there is much pleasure she can give just the way she is?

Shannon Ethridge has something helpful to say on this point: 'I'm...very selective about the women's magazines I pick up because so many of the messages aren't helpful to me. When I read pages and pages of advice on how to be skinnier and look at the pencil-thin models in their underwear, I feel dissatisfied and unhappy with my body. After looking at all of the smooth, tight abdomens scattered throughout the magazine, I can get pretty depressed just looking at myself in the mirror – let alone giving my husband the pleasure of watching me undress. But when I avoid comparing myself and appreciate the strong, healthy body God gave me, I feel much better about my figure to give myself more freely and joyfully to my husband.'[12]

This is not a self-esteem trick to try to convince everyone they are perfectly beautiful. None of us are perfectly beautiful and it is obvious that within our given body type some people are more beautiful than others, just like some mountains are more beautiful than other mountains, some beaches more beautiful than others beaches. But even though each of us has things about us that are not beautiful, we still have a beauty of our own. Just like our favorite spot in the woods, our favorite park or our favorite beach will all have things that are not perfect, and even though there may be other places that are technically more beautiful, yet our favorite place is appealing to us, it is beautiful to us in a way that no other place is, often through the memories we have there. Our bodies and our souls are connected in such a way that what we feel towards a person's soul affects how we

12. Shannon Ethridge, *Every Woman's Battle* (Colorado Springs, CO: WaterBrook Press, 2003), p. 77.

view their body. As 'Dr. John Gray, author of *Mars and Venus in the Bedroom*, says, "When a man is in love and turned on by his wife, he is also totally entranced by the feminine beauty of her body, regardless of where the media would rank it on a scale of one to ten. When he is in love with his wife, he experiences the perfection of her body for him."'[13]

In the next chapter we will see that although physical beauty is a blessing to be enjoyed, yet there is a far greater and more valuable beauty of the inward man. And as David and Diane Vaughan write in *The Beauty of Modesty* '…although we have no biblical standard or ideal for what constitutes physical beauty, we do have a standard of what constitutes moral or inner beauty. That standard is nothing less than the very moral character of our Creator Himself, as reflected in the face of Jesus Christ.'[14]

Whatever physical beauty we have can be taken away from us – and, sadly, age has a way of doing that. It is comforting to know that our true value and beauty comes from the inside and that that can grow and grow as we age. What millions of dollars spent on wrinkle creams, surgeries and hair dyes have failed to accomplish, we as Christians have the secret to: becoming more beautiful as the years go by. When we really believe this, we won't be so obsessed with how our physical bodies compare with those of others. We will see that physical beauty is fool's gold, and who cares if someone has more fool's gold than you do? It's pretty, it sparkles, it excites you for a while, but in the end it's not worth much (Prov. 31:30).

---

13. Linda Dillow and Lorraine Pintus, *Intimate Issues: 21 Questions Christian Women Ask About Sex* (Colorado Springs, CO: WaterBrook Press, 2009), p. 59. They quote Dr. John Gray from his book, *Mars and Venus in the Bedroom* (London: Vermilion, imprint of Penguin Random House UK, 2003).

14. Vaughan, *The Beauty of Modesty*, p. 64.

It takes constantly renewing our minds by God's Word and rejecting the lies implied on billboards and magazine stands everywhere to recognize our natural beauty and be content with it, even though the world scorns it. Worldly thinking involves so much more than we commonly imagine it to be, it is not always obvious sins and heresies, sometimes it is something as simple as believing that our bodies are unattractive.

Feeling Beautiful

There is something in a woman that yearns to feel beautiful. This desire is good, but beauty is a lot like money. It's not how much you have that makes you happy, it's how much you appreciate what you have. There are many extraordinarily beautiful women who never feel pretty enough and there are 'plain Janes' who feel very pretty. God has given you some beauty. It may be more or less than the person next door but it is enough to be happy with. Don't believe that you would be pleased with the way you look if you were just a little prettier. A makeover may make you temporarily happier, just like a raise at work would, but eventually your expectations of what you need to be happy would change and you would go back to feeling like what you had wasn't enough.

Comparisons and competitions are the enemies to contentment. They convince us that we can't feel pretty unless we are prettier than the women around us. We begin to feel threatened when we see a woman prettier than we are. But a true, godly regard for beauty can be happy wherever it finds beauty, whether in oneself, in a sunset or in the woman next door. God has given each of us our own measure of beauty; let's be done with comparisons and competitions and be thankful for the beauty God gives us and equally thankful for the beauty He gives others.

A husband would do well to seek to meet this need by showering his wife with his own attention, delighting in her beauty and praising her appearance. Sadly, many husbands have so feasted their eyes on other women, or even pornography, that they have little to no appreciation for the appearance of their wives. These women can have a particularly hard time feeling beautiful. They are tempted to think that if they could just be prettier their husbands would find them attractive and love them, but that is not true. The problem isn't with their bodies; it's with their husbands' minds. These are very painful situations, more painful than not having a husband at all. If this is you, pray that God will help you to see yourself as He sees you and not as your husband sees you. Seek to have it be enough that God finds you beautiful whether any other man, even your own husband, ever does. The God who has a special place in His heart for those women whose husbands are dead surely has a special place in His heart for those women whose husbands are dead to them.

B. MODESTY UNDERSTANDS THAT SOME BEAUTY IS PRIVATE

Modesty not only appreciates the beauty of the human body, it appreciates the private nature of the greater part of that beauty. Sure, there are parts of our beauty, like our face, that everyone can see, but much of our beauty is not meant for public view. Some beautiful things are meant to be displayed openly – as anyone with a baby will illustrate! But there are also beautiful things that are private, like our sexual lives, which cannot be shared with everyone without losing something priceless. A woman has a God-given desire to share her beauty with a man. It is modest convictions that cause her to hold out to share it in the right time with the right man instead of accepting the more immediate, but ultimately unfulfilling and destructive, pleasure of showing it off now to any man who has eyes to leer. As Jason Evert says, dressing modestly is not hiding our bodies because they are dirty or bad, but 'because you are worth waiting to see.'[15]

---

15. 'Dressing for Love,' Youtube video, 3:16, posted by Jason Evert, May 27, 2011, http://www.youtube.com/watch?v=5_HHcI1A3cw&feature=share.

We've already looked at Song of Solomon 4:12 ('A garden enclosed is my sister, my spouse, a spring shut up, a fountain sealed'), but we haven't yet looked at its context. You might consider stopping now and reading the whole chapter, but here is a summary: the first seven verses praise the beauty of the Shulamite, verses 8-11 talk about how enraptured Solomon is with her beauty and her love, verse 12 speaks of her as a closed garden, the next three verses describe the delights offered in this garden, and the chapter ends with the Shulamite saying: 'Let my beloved come to his garden and eat its pleasant fruits.' A woman's body is a garden of delights for a man, but it should be kept as a private garden, not a public park. Modesty is the fence, charming as white pickets and daunting as barbed wire, which keeps it from being trampled by every man that comes along, saving it for her beloved alone. As for her beloved, he enjoys her garden all the more in the knowledge that it is his unique privilege to enjoy the fullness of its beauty.

C. Modesty is content to be beautiful to one man

Carolyn Mahaney makes an important point when she says that while it is our culture which 'puts forth a false standard of beauty and a false message about beauty', yet it is 'ultimately the wickedness already resident in the human heart... [that] motivates us to believe such lies and pursue them.'[16]

Perhaps the sin that makes us most susceptible to these lies is the sin of being discontent with being beautiful in the eyes of one man only. In a later chapter we will talk about how the desire to be seen as beautiful is part of the sexual makeup of a woman. As with other sexual desires, when this desire is directed to one's spouse, it is righteous and lovely, but when it is directed at others, it is sinful.

16. Mahaney, 'True Beauty' in *Biblical Womanhood,* p. 36.

The need to have other men find you attractive is not just sinful, it is hurtful. If you need other men to find you attractive in order to feel beautiful, you will always be insecure. It will be hard to appreciate the beauty God has given you. How freeing it can be to enjoy your husband's attraction to you without ever worrying what any other man thinks of your appearance. If you were to boil down female modesty to its essence, you might find that it is a delight in one's beauty that seeks to thrill one's husband and one's husband only.

For the same reason, a husband's delight in his wife must not devolve into parading her beauty Artaxerses-like before others[17]. A woman's beauty is not a trophy for her husband to flaunt smugly. Obviously others will see much of her beauty, she does not, after all, live behind convent walls, but a man should not go out of his way to make her seen in order to feed his own ego. It should be enough for a man to know how beautiful his wife is without needing other men to be admiring her too. Despite what Facebook would seem to indicate, romance was not meant to be a spectator sport.

Dannah Gresh tells young girls, '*Your* body can really drive a guy crazy. And that's what God intended. Check out Proverbs 5:18-19 where it tells a man to 'rejoice in the wife of your youth.... May you ever be *captivated* by her love.' That word captivated would be better translated 'intoxicated' since that's what the Hebrew writer was trying to suggest.... Again and again, the Bible reconfirms that this intoxication is only to be shared with one guy... and after you're married. Until then, it's under wraps... a secret to be shared with your husband. Sure, you could 'have many men,' but God says 'just one.' Until then, the fullest secrets of the incredible masterpiece of your body are

---

17. Esther 1:10-11.

to be your unique secret....You were created to express God's beauty, and if His plan is for you to marry one day, part of your purpose is to "intoxicate" one man with that beauty.'[18]

And what if we're not married? Nancy DeMoss Wolgemuth says to single women, and it has applications for single men as well, 'you have only one person to please: The Lord should be the object of your pursuit for beauty (1 Cor. 7:34). All your thoughts, motives, and actions related to beauty should be for the eyes of One and One only.'[19] As Christians we all have Christ for our husband, but I Corinthians 7:32-34 says that singles are able to live for their heavenly husband in a way that those who are married cannot: 'He who is unmarried cares for the things of the Lord – how he may please the Lord. But he who is married cares about the things of the world – how he may please his wife. There is a difference between a wife and a virgin. The unmarried woman cares about the things of the Lord, that she may be holy both in body and in spirit. But she who is married cares about the things of the world – how she may please her husband.'

The desire of a woman to share her beauty with a man and of a man to revel in a woman's beauty is as deep and as real as the desire for intimacy, companionship and children. The fact that we have a heavenly bridegroom does not obliterate these desires. But it can help us to think less of what we don't have and to remind ourselves more of what we do have, because what we have in Christ is priceless and 1 Corinthians tells singles that they can be particularly devoted to Him and His service.

Marriage is so beautiful and special because it is a picture of something beautiful and special, that of the relationship between Christ and the church. This picture of marriage is but a poor

---

18. Dannah Gresh, *Secret Keeper: The Delicate Power of Modesty* (Moody, 2005) pp. 20-21, 24.

19. Mahaney, 'True Beauty' in *Biblical Womanhood*, p. 40.

imitation of the real thing and yet we can be so consumed with the imitation that we don't appreciate the original. What would we think of a woman who had a diamond and though she liked it well enough and thought it was rather pretty, yet what she really wanted was a picture of a diamond and couldn't be happy until she had the picture and envied everyone else who did have the picture? Wouldn't we want to tell her, 'Um, look, don't you see that diamond you have there? Isn't it altogether lovely? Isn't it fairer than ten thousands of pictures?'

What is more, the very fact that singles are freed from the distractions of the picture means that they can devote themselves more wholeheartedly to the diamond. It is true that now we see this diamond through a veil darkly, it is true that as long as we live in this body the desires for a spouse will always be there, but let us look up and let us look forward, forward to the day when the veil will be taken away and we will see Him face to face, the One who is altogether lovely and fairer than ten thousand, to the day when people will no longer be given into marriage because the picture will have no purpose now that the reality is clearly seen. That day is coming and it is coming fast when marriage will hold no attraction to us because it has been so fully swallowed up by that which so far surpasses it: Jesus Christ.

> The King there in His beauty, without a veil is seen:
> It were a well spent journey, though seven deaths lay between:
> The Lamb with His fair army, doth on Mount Zion stand,
> And glory – glory dwelleth in Immanuel's land.
>
> O Christ, He is the fountain, the deep, sweet well of love!
> The streams on earth I've tasted more deep I'll drink above:
> There to an ocean fullness His mercy doth expand,
> And glory, glory dwelleth in Immanuel's land.[20]

20. Anne R. Cousin, 'The Sands of Time are Sinking' (1857).

5: The Relative Importance of Beauty

Though God made people, and women in particular, beautiful, the Bible exhorts us, and women in particular, not to give inordinate attention to the way we look. In an earlier chapter we saw that modesty can be divided into two types: one that is primarily sexual and is about what parts of the body one exposes, and one that is primarily materialistic and is about extravagance in money and time spent on one's appearance. These two aspects are closely related, those who lavish attention on the way they look are more likely to reveal their bodies provocatively. Both extravagant immodesty and sexual immodesty have the same root: a desire to gain attention and admiration through one's appearance.[1] Because the bodies of women are some of the most

1. 'Why do you desire to be so fine, neat, or excessively comely? Is it not to draw the eyes and observations of men upon you? And to what end? Is it not to be thought either rich or beautiful or of a handsome person? To what end desire you these thoughts of men? Do you not know that this desire is pride itself? You must needs be somebody, and fain you would

beautiful sights in the world, dressing modestly will hide much of that beauty, resulting in less attention, less admiration from men around her. If a woman thinks her physical beauty is the best thing she has going for her, then she's going to resist anything that might hide it or detract from it. On the other hand, if she views beauty as the Bible views it, realizing that physical beauty is empty and fleeting and internal beauty is far more meaningful and far more lasting, then convincing her to dress modestly will come much more easily.

Interestingly enough, the Bible addresses materialistic modesty much more clearly than it does sexual modesty in

---

be observed and valued!... I hope you know that pride is the devil's sin, the firstborn of all iniquity, and that which the God of heaven abhors!... Too oft it [this desire to have others think us especially beautiful] shows a pang of *lust* as well as pride... it is plainly a wooing, alluring act. It is not for nothing that they would [eagerly] be eyed and be thought comely or fair in others' eyes! They want something: you may conjecture *what*!.... the more a man desireth esteem, the less he deserves it. You tell the world by your attire that you desire it-even as plainly and foolishly as if you should say to the folks in the streets, "I pray think well of me and take me for a handsome, comely person, and for one that is above the common sort." Would you not *laugh* at one that should make such a request to you? Why, what do you less when by your attire you beg estimation from them? For what, I pray you, *should* we esteem you? *Is it for your clothes?* Why, I can put a silver lace upon a [mop] or a silken coat on a post or a [donkey]. *Is it for your comely bodies?* Why, a wicked Absalom was beautiful, and the basest harlots have had as much of this as you!.... *Is it for your virtues that you would be esteemed?* Why pride is the greatest enemy to virtue and as great a deformity to the soul as the pox is to the body.... Either let honor come without begging or be without it.... In the eyes of a wise and gracious man, a poor self-denying, humble, patient, heavenly Christian is worth a thousand of these painted posts and peacocks.' –Richard Baxter, 'A Treatise of Self-Denial' in *Baxter's PracticalWorks, Vol. 3* (Soli Deo Gloria), quoted in *Free Grace Broadcaster* no. 216 (Summer 2011): pp. 32-34.

clothing. When the Bible encourages women to modesty in 1 Timothy 2:9 it seems to have this aspect primarily in view since it addresses 'braided hair or gold or pearls or costly clothing' and not 'short skirts or low cut blouses.' This is a good place to ask why. Why does the Bible speak more directly about dressing ostentatiously than it does about dressing revealingly?

Though the Bible was written for all people in all times, it was also written in the context of the people of that time. In those days to dress seductively was to overdo the cosmetics and clothing and jewelry in an eye-catching way. Showing a lot of skin wasn't as much of an issue, this is not to say it never happened, only that it wasn't as common. The Bible is sufficient for everything we face, but that doesn't mean everything is addressed by name (more about this in the next chapter). This is the same reason why the Bible says more about masters and slaves than about employers and employees and why it deals thoroughly with false teachings of that day and doesn't by name condemn false teachings in our day. The problems they faced with modesty in their day may not be the same exact problems we have in our day, but there are parallels and lessons to be learned. The same heart attitude that will keep us from dressing extravagantly will also keep us from dressing seductively.

A. A Biblical Perspective on Appearance

Let's take a moment to look at some of the verses where the Bible talks about beauty in a positive way:

> 'She makes tapestry for herself; her clothing is fine linen and purple.' (Prov. 31:22)

> 'The royal daughter is all glorious within the palace; her clothing is woven with gold. She shall be brought to the King in robes of many colors…' (Ps. 45:13-14a)

The Song of Solomon, as we have already seen, is full of celebrations of physical beauty.

Creation around us clearly shows us that God loves beauty. We've even seen that the word *kosmios* (where we get our word cosmos) conveys, not only an idea of orderliness, but also one of adornment. In fact, Matthew 6:28-30 tells us that God has so adorned the lilies of the field that not even Solomon in all his glory can match their beauty. From the example of the lilies we see both that God loves beauty and that beauty is more often found in simplicity than in extravagance.[2]

John A. James sums it up well: 'To reject all ideas and efforts to add the fair to the good, the beautiful to the useful, would be to oppose and not imitate, to condemn and not to approve, the works of the great Creator.'[3]

The Bible is, however, also very clear on the limitations of beauty. In fact, it seems to go to greater lengths to make this point, perhaps because we are more prone to err on this side. It comes pretty naturally to think that beauty is good and desirable, our tendency is to put too great a value on it, not too little of a value.

> 'But the Lord said to Samuel, "Do not look at his appearance or at his physical stature, because I have refused him. For the Lord does not see as man sees; for man looks at the outward appearance, but the Lord looks at the heart."' (1 Sam. 16:7)

> 'As a ring of gold in a swine's snout, so is a lovely woman who lacks discretion.' (Prov. 11:22)

---

2. Edith Schaeffer in her book *The Hidden Art of Homemaking* picks up on this theme.

3. John Angell James, *Female Piety: A Young Woman's Friend and Guide* (Morgan, PA: Soli Deo Gloria Publications, 1999), p. 221 [originally published in 1860].

Speaking of the coming destruction of Judah, God says, 'Though you clothe yourself with crimson, though you adorn yourself with ornaments of gold, though you enlarge your eyes with paint, in vain you will make yourself fair; your lovers will despise you; they will seek your life' (Jer. 4:30b).

Describing the coming destruction of the tribe of Ephraim, God says, '...whose glorious beauty is a fading flower...' (Isa. 28:1).

The book of Ezekiel is filled with judgments against various cities, judgments which often include a description of their beauty and how it will be destroyed. Tyre is one example:

> 'You were the seal of perfection, full of wisdom and perfect in beauty. You were in Eden, the garden of God; every precious stone was your covering: the sardius, topaz, and diamond, beryl, onyx, and jasper, sapphire, turquoise, and emerald with gold.... Your heart was lifted up because of your beauty; you corrupted your wisdom for the sake of your splendor; I cast you to the ground, I laid you before kings, that they might gaze at you.... All who knew you among the peoples are astonished at you; you have become a horror, and shall be no more forever.' (Ezek. 28:12b-19)

Speaking of the great harlot,it is said:

> 'The woman was arrayed in purple and scarlet, and adorned with gold and precious stones and pearls, having in her hand a golden cup full of abominations and the filthiness of her fornication.' (Rev. 17:4)

Proverbs 31:30 reminds us of what is truly valuable: 'Charm is deceitful and beauty is passing, but a woman who fears the Lord, she shall be praised.'

Carolyn Mahaney says it well when she writes in *Biblical Womanhood in the Home*: '[A woman with physical] beauty makes a fleeting, momentary impression. But a woman who cultivates inner beauty, who fears God and lives to serve others, makes a difference in people's lives. Her beauty makes a lasting impact on the lives she touches. Godly, inner beauty makes an indelible mark on the lives of others and glorifies God.'[4]

When looking at the places where appearance or beauty is mentioned, there is a noticeable difference between the Old and New Testament[5]. In the Old Testament we are told that David was ruddy, good-looking, and had bright eyes, that Joseph was handsome in form and appearance, that Daniel and his friends were good-looking and without blemish, that Esther was lovely and beautiful, that Sarah was of beautiful countenance, that Tamar was lovely, we are told that Saul was tall and Absalom had

---

4. Mahaney, 'True Beauty' in *Biblical Womanhood,* p. 38.

5. William Hendriksen comments on Ephesians 1:3 concerning how we are blessed with every spiritual blessings in heavenly places in Christ, saying, 'While it is *not* true that the Old Testament regards material goods as being of higher value than spiritual, for the contrary is clearly taught in such passages as Genesis 15:1; 17:7; Psalms 37:16; 73:25; Proverbs 3:13, 14; 8:11, 17-19; 17:1; 19:1, 22; 28:6; Isaiah 30:15; cf. Hebrews. 11:9, 10, it is true, nevertheless, that between the two Testaments there is a difference of degree in the fulness [sic] of detail with which earthly or physical blessings are described (Exod. 20:12; Deut. 28:1-8; Neh. 9:21-25). God is ever the wise Pedagogue who takes his children by the hand and knows that in the old dispensation, "when Israel is a child" it needs this circumstantial description of earthly values in order that by means of these as symbols (e.g., earthly Canaan is the symbol of the heavenly), it may rise to the appreciation of the spiritual (cf. I Cor. 15:46). The New Testament, while by no means deprecating earthly blessings (Matt. 6:11; I Tim. 4:3, 4), places all the emphasis on the spiritual (2 Cor. 4:18), and it may well have been that in order to emphasize this difference between the old and the new dispensation it is here stated that the God and Father of our Lord Jesus Christ blessed us with every *spiritual* blessing.' – *New Testament Commentary: Exposition of Ephesians* (Grand Rapids, MI: Baker Book House, 1967), p. 73.

thick hair. But when we come to the New Testament, what do we know of Paul's appearance? Or Peter's? Or Lydia's or Mary's or Martha's? The only thing it mentions, that I can think of, is that Zaccheus was a wee little man! Even when it comes to Jesus, the only description we have is the one given in Isaiah. Though it may not be a strictly physical description, it is a general description of Him in His humanity and it is likely that His physical appearance was in line with it: 'He has no form or comeliness; and when we see him, there is no beauty that we should desire him' (Isa. 53:2).

The Old Testament emphasized prosperity and physical beauty in a way that the New Testament doesn't. The Old Testament gave instructions for a magnificent temple, the New Testament believers met in homes. In the Old Testament the norm was for the righteous to be wealthy, in the New Testament the norm is for the righteous to be persecuted. We have greater light in the New Testament and so we are expected to walk more by faith and more in view of heavenly realities. This was certainly the case in the Old Testament as well, as the examples of Abraham and Job prove, but it is even more so in the New Testament. Not only do we have greater light, we also have a greater example. Jesus wasn't wealthy, wasn't handsome, didn't have an easy, cushy life, didn't receive much of the praise of men, didn't die a quiet death being full of years. If our master had it thus, what right do we have to expect anything better (Matt. 10:24-25)? In striking a balance between a wholesome appreciation for beauty and an unwholesome preoccupation with beauty, we should keep in mind that it may be different for us living under the New Covenant than it was for believers under the Old Covenant.

B. Comparing and Contrasting Two Verses on Female Adornment

Let's look at two verses in the New Testament which give us a good balance:

> 'Do not let your adorning be external – the braiding of hair and the putting on of gold jewelry, or the clothing you wear – but let your adorning be the hidden person of the heart with the imperishable beauty of a gentle and quiet spirit, which in God's sight is very precious.' (1 Pet. 3:3-4, ESV)

> [I desire] 'that the women adorn themselves in modest apparel, with propriety and moderation, not with braided hair or gold or pearls or costly clothing, but, which is proper for women professing godliness, with good works.' (1 Tim. 2:9-10)

It is interesting that Peter and Paul were on the same page about what a woman's beauty should not be. They both mention braided hair, gold and clothing, while Paul throws in pearls as well. This likely is the result of living in the same culture and seeing the same excesses. Braided hair can be very simple, but in Bible times it was anything but simple as the following description illustrates:

> 'But what about these *braids* which were popular in the world of Paul's day? No expense was spared to make them dazzling. They actually sparkled. The braids were fastened by jewelled tortoise-shell combs, or by pins of ivory or silver. Or the pins were of bronze with jewelled heads, the more varied and expensive the better. The pin-heads often consisted of miniature images (an animal, a human hand, an idol, the female figure, etc.). *Braids*, in those days, often represented *fortunes*. They were articles of luxury! The Christian woman is warned not to indulge in such extravagance.

> 'Similarly,' William Hendriksen continues 'a woman who is a believer must not try to make herself conspicuous by a vain display of ornaments of *gold*. Also, she will not yearn for *pearls*, obtained (at that time) from the Persian Gulf or from the Indian Ocean. These were often fabulously priced and thus way beyond the purchasing power of the average church-member....
>
> 'A woman of faith will not (at least *should not*) crave *costly garments*, for example a most expensive and showy robe. The robe or mantle worn by the lady resembled a man's toga. However, it was often the product of finer workmanship, and was characterized by richer ornamentation, and greater color-variation.'[6]

Some people believe that these verses teach that a woman should never wear jewelry or braid her hair. But the emphasis is on extravagance and so much of today's jewelry isn't even real, costing as little as a couple of dollars and so many of today's braids are very simple, taking as little as a few minutes. As John A. James wrote, 'The prohibition seems to be comparative rather than absolute, and contains an injunction to be far more attentive to the ornaments of the soul than to those of the body. "I will have mercy, and not sacrifice" means, "I prefer mercy to sacrifice."'[7] Some may want to be on the safe side and forgo these things, that's not a problem as long as it does not become a substitute for obeying the real message of this text: we should focus on those things which are lasting. It profits us nothing if we obey the negative command, but neglect to obey the positive command.

One difference between the two texts is that Paul is speaking in the context of women in the church (1 Tim. 3:1 'This is

6. William Hendriksen, *New Testament Commentary: Exposition of I and II Thessalonians, I and II Timothy and Titus* (Grand Rapids, MI: Baker Book House, 1979), pp. 107-108.

7. James, *Female Piety,* p. 222.

a faithful saying: If a man desires the position of a bishop, he desires a good work') and Peter is speaking in the context of women in the home (1 Peter 3:1 'Wives, likewise, be submissive to your own husbands'). From this we learn that this principle applies everywhere, it is not just something for the church or just something for the home.

An interesting difference in the two passages is that Paul tells women to adorn themselves with good works and Peter tells women to adorn themselves with a gentle and quiet spirit. We know that the Holy Spirit inspired both of them to say what they said and so we realize that both are true and that both are important for us to remember. It's not enough to be active doing good works if we neglect our own hearts. Nor is it enough to be so focused on our own spiritual lives that we give no thought to doing good to those around us. In between these two extremes of mysticism and activism lies the place where Christians can find their true beauty. A hymn by F. H. Allen captures this balance, or should we say this unity, so picturesquely:

> 'Within the Veil,' His fragrance poured upon thee,
> Without the Veil, that fragrance shed abroad;
> 'Within the Veil,' His hand shall tune the music
> Which sounds on earth the praises of Thy Lord.'

6: Christian Liberty and Modesty

As we look at what modesty is, we should also look at what it is that governs the standards of modesty. Most people will agree that modesty in general is a black-and-white issue. Modesty is right and immodesty, whatever that is, is wrong. But when it comes to the specific standards of modesty, what type of issue are we looking at? Many people in our day say that it is a matter of Christian liberty. There is reason to believe that it is hazy thinking about Christian liberty in general, and how it relates to modesty in particular, that is responsible for much of the immodesty that overtook the church in the twentieth century.

Christian liberty has many facets, including our freedom from the bondage of sin and from the necessity of observing the ceremonial law; this chapter will focus on two facets which are the most relevant to the question of modesty: our liberty in things indifferent and our liberty from the doctrines and commandments of men.

A. Our Liberty in Things Indifferent

In his *Institutes*, Calvin says of this facet of Christian liberty: '… we are not bound before God to any observance of external things which are in themselves indifferent, ("adiafora") but that we are now at full liberty either to use or omit them.' He goes on to apply it to the use of quality fabric and quality food. His point is that such things are not evil in and of themselves, quoting Paul in Romans 14:14: 'I know, that there is nothing unclean of itself: but to him that esteems anything to be unclean, to him it is unclean.' Calvin goes on to say that we must always use moderation in our enjoyment of God's good gifts, that is, we are not at liberty to become gluttons.

It is this liberty in things indifferent that is often referenced when people say that entertainment choices, dress, etc. are a matter of Christian liberty. To evaluate that application let's take a closer look at what Romans 14, the passage Calvin is rooting this doctrine in, says:

> Romans 14: 'Receive one who is weak in the faith, but not to disputes over doubtful things. For one believes he may eat all things, but he who is weak eats only vegetables. Let not him who eats despise him who does not eat, and let not him who does not eat judge him who eats; for God has received him.… let us not judge one another anymore, but rather resolve this, not to put a stumbling block or a cause to fall in our brother's way. I know and am convinced by the Lord Jesus that there is nothing unclean of itself; but to him who considers anything to be unclean, to him it is unclean. Yet if your brother is grieved because of your food, you are no longer walking in love. Do not destroy with your food the one for whom Christ died.… All things indeed are pure, but it is evil for the man who eats with offense. It is good neither to eat meat nor drink wine nor do anything by which your brother stumbles or is offended or

> is made weak. Do you have faith? Have it to yourself before God. Happy is he who does not condemn himself in what he approves. But he who doubts is condemned if he eats, because he does not eat from faith; for whatever is not from faith is sin.'

In understanding how Romans 14 applies to our lives today we must first determine what types of things it is speaking of. If, for example, we were to apply these principles to something like adultery or murder, the results would be obviously disastrous. Less obvious, but potentially still disastrous, would be the results if these principles were applied to other things they were not meant to govern. Many people believe that Paul is speaking of the ceremonial law and the person who is weak in faith is still trying to practice the ceremonial law. I believe this is the most likely interpretation especially because of the use of the word unclean. Calvin believed that these principles govern the use of things which are external. This is closely related to the ceremonial law which also governed many things external, but broadens the scope a bit. Some today teach that it applies to anything not directly forbidden in God's Word. We'll deal with that question in the next section.

Romans 14 itself describes the things as 'doubtful.' This means that it's not clear in everyone's mind what is right and wrong. It also presents the one who has the doubts as being weak in the faith which shows us that it is speaking of times when the doubts are not valid, times when something acceptable is wrongly thought to be sinful. This is important to recognize because if we were to try to take these principles and apply them to times when the doubts are good and right then we marginalize those who are seeking to follow the Bible. If, to give another obvious example, we were to try to use this chapter to reconcile someone who believed it was fine to have an abortion and someone who had doubts about it, we would be undermining God's Word.

What should be clear is that whatever these doubtful things are, they are innocent and harmless, and whatever we want to treat as a Romans 14 issue we must first make very sure is also innocent and harmless. The Bible in a multitude of places teaches that the foods we eat do not defile a man (e.g. Matt. 15:11, 'Not what goes into the mouth defiles a man; but what comes out of the mouth, this defiles a man'). Food goes in and goes out without being inherently sinful. But the Bible treats what we put into our minds very differently from what we put into our mouths and we must as well. The Bible gives us many commands about our thoughts, Philippians 4:8 being the most comprehensive command[1]. The thoughts we put into our minds are not harmless and indifferent, they will affect us one way or another. What we think about gets written on our hearts. In whatever areas we want to apply Romans 14, we must not use it as the governing principle to something which has such a huge potential to adversely affect our spiritual lives.

Some have argued that movies, TV, books, music CDs and clothes are all external things and cannot be inherently immoral. As physical objects, this is true. If we are using a book to press flowers it doesn't necessarily matter if it is *Pilgrim's Progress* or *Playboy*. But once we take up a book to read, it has ceased to be a thing external; it is now being internalized and put into our minds and hearts. It is at this point that these things cease to be mere physical objects, cease to be things indifferent and begin to have moral implications, good or bad. While it is true that we have no definite rules about which books are good or bad and that it is possible at certain times a book that is good for

1. 'Finally, brethren, whatever things are true, whatever things are noble, whatever things are just, whatever things are pure, whatever things are lovely, whatever things are of good report, if there is any virtue and if there is anything praiseworthy – meditate on these things.'

one person will be bad for another, we can never afford to be indifferent about what we put into our minds.

In a different way, the same is true of clothes, as physical objects they are completely neutral, if we are using a piece of clothing to make a quilt it doesn't matter whether it is a burqa or a bikini, but once we wear them out in public they are rousing thoughts in the minds of those who see us and have the very real potential to do great harm. Modesty is certainly very doubtful, Christians disagree over what they should and shouldn't wear, but it is not harmless and indifferent, it is not something that goes in the mouth and ends up in the toilet.

In fact, if movies and dress were matters indifferent, then, according to Romans 14, the person who has any convictions regarding the movies they watch or the clothes they wear, is weak in the faith. In such a case it should be expected that the weak brother would eventually grow in strength and faith and begin to enjoy the full range of entertainment and fashion. This would be to say that the apostle Paul, who understood his Christian liberty better than anyone, would watch any movies and read any books as long as no one else was around to stumble at his liberty. Can you really see Paul alone in his hotel room enjoying the adult entertainment channels? But if it is a thing indifferent, then it is only the weakness of our faith that has trouble imagining this.

Now, to be fair, when people say that entertainment or dress is a matter of Christian liberty, they very seldom mean all entertainment or all dress. Everyone will draw the line someplace different, usually somewhere far away from what they themselves are comfortable watching and what they themselves are comfortable wearing, and say that everything across that line is definitely bad. But the whole point of something being indifferent is that you don't have to decide whether it is good or bad. You don't have to wonder whether this meat crosses the line into bad meat. It can't be bad because it is only meat! You don't have to wonder if this or that ceremonial law is still binding – none of them are binding! If there are some movies that are bad, some clothes that are immodest to wear in public, only we don't know for sure exactly which ones they are, the one thing we do know is that the issue is not a Romans 14 type of issue.

One more thing to note from Romans 14 is the type of weakness that is in view. The person who is made to stumble is weak in the faith; the Bible commentator Matthew Henry says that he is 'mistaken and misinformed.' His problem is that he does not understand the liberty he has in Christ and is treating innocent things as if they were sinful. The danger is that if those who know their liberty are not careful, they can cause him to follow their example against his own conscience and thus sin, not because what he does is wrong but because he thinks it is wrong. This passage is often misapplied to modesty – women are told to remember their weak brethren and dress so as not to be a stumbling block – but the weaknesses are not the same. In regards to immodesty, if a man stumbles it is not due to a *weakness of knowledge,* it is due to a *weakness of human nature.* It is not as if it were perfectly good for him to lust after a woman's body but he is 'mistaken and misinformed' and so he sins against his conscience when he gazes on a scantily dressed woman. No, it is that his human nature is prone to lust and immodest dress arouses that lust and lures him to sin. Lust is certainly not a thing indifferent, it is sin whether a person thinks it is or not. Many men have no qualms about lust and would be happy for a woman to reveal herself to their eager eyes, but women do not have the liberty to give them that pleasure just because it does not hurt their consciences. Though immodest dress can be an occasion for a man stumbling, it is not the type of stumbling Romans 14 is addressing. It is not a stumbling that can be helped by growing in knowledge and faith and finding that the thing assumed sinful was permissible all along.

In saying this, I would not have anyone get the idea that we can be careless about how our dress affects others as long as we are sure it is objectively modest. Though it is not the type of issue Romans 14 is addressing, we can glean from this and other passages in God's Word that we should love our neighbor as ourselves and treat our brethren as people for whom Christ has died. Modesty itself is not a matter indifferent, but there are many clothes that are modest and which of those we wear **is** a matter indifferent and we should be willing to give up our right to wear the modest clothes we would prefer in order to wear those that are considerate of others. The circumstances may not always require this self-denial, but we should always be willing.

B. Our Liberty from the Doctrines and Commandments of Men

The Baptist Confession of Faith of 1689[2] contains a chapter called 'Of Christian Liberty and Liberty of Conscience'. Paragraph two of that chapter deals with another facet of our liberty in Christ, often called liberty of conscience:

> 'God alone is Lord of the conscience, and hath left it free from the doctrines and commandments of men which are in any thing contrary to his Word, or not contained in it. So that to believe such doctrines, or obey such commands out of conscience, is to betray true liberty of conscience; and the requiring of an implicit faith, and absolute and blind obedience, is to destroy liberty of conscience and reason also.'

---

2. This confession is largely modeled after the *Westminster Confession*, the main differences being in regards to Baptistic doctrines. This confession would go on to be embraced and reprinted by Charles Spurgeon. In our day it is often held to by Reformed Baptists.

Let's begin by looking at some verses that deal with this aspect of our Christian liberty:

After calling the scribes and Pharisees hypocrites when they criticized His disciples for not washing their hands before eating bread while at the same time they undermined God's commandment to honor father and mother through their teaching of devoting to God money that should have been spent on helping their parents, Jesus says that Isaiah was speaking of them when he said:

> 'These people draw near to Me with their mouth, and honor Me with their lips, but their heart is far from Me. And in vain they worship Me, teaching as doctrines **the commandments of men**.' (Matt. 15:8-9)

> 'Therefore, if you died with Christ from the basic principles of the world, why, as though living in the world, do you subject yourself to regulations – Do not touch, do not taste, do not handle,' which all concern things which perish with the using- according to **the commandments and doctrines of men**?' (Col. 2:20-22)

Speaking of the Judaizers who taught that Christians still needed to obey the ceremonial law, Paul writes in Titus 1:13-14: 'Therefore rebuke them sharply, that they may be sound in the faith, not giving heed to Jewish fables and **commandments of men** who turn from the truth.'

These passages are all clear that no man is free to add to the commandments that God has given. It is most likely that these passages are dealing with people who were teaching that Christians are still subject to the ceremonial law which God had done away with in Christ. But if it is wrong to teach commandments that God had once given and then rescinded, how much more wrong is it to teach commandments that God never gave?

This liberty from the doctrines and commandments of men is rooted in the *completion of Scripture*. God has revealed His mind in the Bible, it is complete, and He has forbidden man to add to what He has said. It is also rooted in the *sufficiency of Scripture*. The Bible contains everything we need to know to follow God and please Him, it is sufficient to guide us in everything we face and so there is no need for man to add to it. This liberty is also rooted in the *uniqueness of God*. God alone is infallible and can reveal truth infallibly; man is not and cannot. God alone is sovereign and has the authority to give commands which are binding on all men everywhere; man is not and does not. These truths are crucial and we cannot lose hold of them without losing the liberty Christ died to bring us.

Unfortunately, what has happened in many places is that people have taken this liberty from the doctrines and commandments of men and have said that it includes anything not *explicitly* forbidden or commanded in God's Word. The Bible does not give exact standards of modesty so therefore, some say, modesty must be a matter of Christian liberty, one person's standards are as good as another's as long as they are 'prayerfully considered.' Movies are never mentioned at all in God's Word so therefore they too, the thinking goes, must be a matter of Christian liberty. I trust we will see that this interpretation is unsustainable, for there are all sorts of things that are not explicitly forbidden or commanded but yet are undeniably wrong or right in the light of other Biblical principles and teachings.

Shannon Ethridge wrote a helpful and insightful book, *Every Woman's Battle*, about the sexual struggles of women and some of the excellent observations she makes will be quoted throughout this book, but it is this wrong thinking about Christian liberty (and the law) that causes her to ask, 'While it is lawful for a single woman to flirt with a married man, is it the loving thing to do?'[3] Did you catch that? She believes that it is lawful for a single woman to flirt with a married man! After all, the Bible nowhere explicitly forbids extramarital flirting. The question, she says, is 'Is it loving?' and she goes on to say that it is not. I certainly don't want to leave anyone with the impression that Ethridge condones extramarital flirting, that is the direct opposite of her intention, only to give an example of where such thinking of Christian liberty could lead us.

Is this teaching (and Ethridge is far from the only one who says such things) harmless since in the end she believes that we should not flirt with married people? Does it matter whether we believe something is lawful or not as long as we say it is not loving?[4] Yes, it does matter, because once we believe that objectively, in the Bible, there is nothing to forbid a particular practice, then all we are left with are subjective feelings and subjectivity is much more easily molded to fit our desires. When we really want to do something, and we are told that there is nothing inherently wrong in it, it is pretty easy to convince ourselves that it is permissible for us in our situation.

This is also a dangerous teaching because whether something feels wrong or not, feels unloving or not, is greatly influenced by the world around us. It is probable that this thinking is partly to blame for how the church is growing increasingly worldly. Every generation is influenced by its culture and as society drifts (or runs) further from God, each generation is being

---

3. Ethridge, *Every Woman's Battle,* p. 28.

4. 'The practical effect of making all ethical decisions logical deductions or inferences from the law of love is to reduce man's need for divine instruction. He needs to be told only one thing, to "love", and he will work all the rest out himself.' – Noel Weeks, *The Sufficiency of Scripture* (Edinburgh: Banner of Truth Trust, 1988), p. 12.

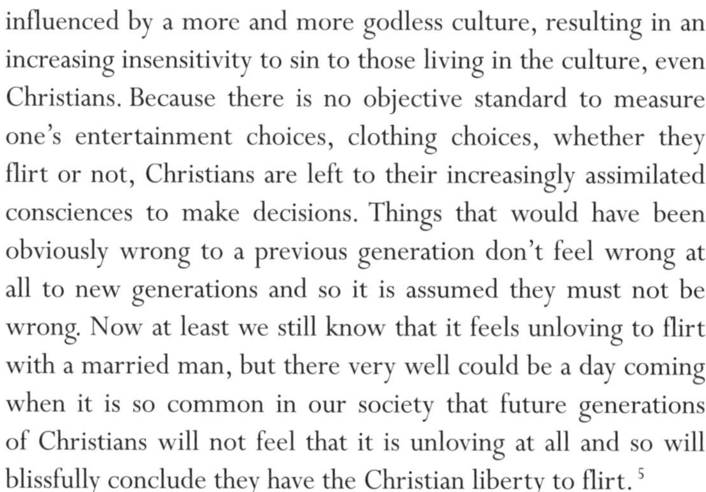

influenced by a more and more godless culture, resulting in an increasing insensitivity to sin to those living in the culture, even Christians. Because there is no objective standard to measure one's entertainment choices, clothing choices, whether they flirt or not, Christians are left to their increasingly assimilated consciences to make decisions. Things that would have been obviously wrong to a previous generation don't feel wrong at all to new generations and so it is assumed they must not be wrong. Now at least we still know that it feels unloving to flirt with a married man, but there very well could be a day coming when it is so common in our society that future generations of Christians will not feel that it is unloving at all and so will blissfully conclude they have the Christian liberty to flirt. [5]

It is undeniable that the Bible nowhere condemns by name flirting with another's spouse and, as we have seen, we have no right to say something is sinful if the Bible does not, but is a direct, explicit commandment the only biblical way we can know something is sinful?

Noel Weeks writes, 'One…meets an ignoring of general principles in the common argument that the absence of a specific command means that there is no Biblical teaching on a subject. Paul who built an argument for paying evangelists from a law on oxen had a far better appreciation of the structure of Biblical law.

5. 'Could this film be shown in heaven? If my answer is no, there's no way I'm picking this video off the shelf at Blockbuster….I really have only one rule: whatever pollutes is off-limits. But I'm very careful to let the Bible tell me what pollutes. Consulting the Bible is important because if we are as desensitized to sensuality (as appears to be the case), then it's critical that we recast Scripture into the central role of our entertainment decisions. Otherwise, we'll be polluting ourselves without even realizing it.' – Stephen Arterburn, Fred Stoeker and Mike Yorkey, *Every Single Man's Battle: Staying on the Path of Sexual Purity* (Colorado Springs, CO: WaterBrook Press, 2005), pp. 52-53.

He did not need a specific commandment on pay for evangelists because, as he himself says, God did not give the command just for the sake of oxen' (1 Cor. 9:9, 10).[6]

Weeks says that in addition to giving us specific rules and regulations, commands also teach us principles which can be applied to things not directly addressed. The writers of the *Westminster Larger Catechism* understood this truth. In question ninety-nine they gave eight rules for correctly understanding how to apply the Ten Commandments. Rule number six was: 'That under one sin or duty, all of the same kind are forbidden or commanded; together with all the **causes, means, occasions, and appearances thereof, and provocations thereunto**.'[7] So when they dealt with the commandment forbidding adultery, they believed it was saying more than don't have sex with someone you are not married to. Note the many applications they derived from this one commandment:

Question 138: What are the duties required in the seventh commandment?

Answer: The duties required in the seventh commandment are, chastity in body, mind, affections, words, and behavior; and the preservation of it in ourselves and others; watchfulness over the eyes and all the senses; temperance, keeping of chaste company, modesty in apparel; marriage by those that have not the gift of continency, conjugal love, and cohabitation; diligent labor in our callings; shunning all occasions of uncleanness, and resisting temptations thereunto.

Question 139: What are the sins forbidden in the seventh commandment?

---

6. Noel Weeks, *The Sufficiency of Scripture* (Edinburgh: Banner of Truth Trust, 1988), p. 12.

7. Bolding mine.

Answer: The sins forbidden in the seventh commandment, besides the neglect of the duties required, are, adultery, fornication, rape, incest, sodomy, and all unnatural lusts; all unclean imaginations, thoughts, purposes, and affections; all corrupt or filthy communications, or listening thereunto; **wanton looks, impudent or light behavior**[8], immodest apparel; prohibiting of lawful, and dispensing with unlawful marriages; allowing, tolerating, keeping of stews [houses of prostitution], and resorting to them; entangling vows of single life, undue delay of marriage; having more wives or husbands than one at the same time; unjust divorce, or desertion; idleness, gluttony, drunkenness, unchaste company; lascivious songs, books, pictures, dancings, stage plays; and all other provocations to, or acts of uncleanness, either in ourselves or others.

The writers of this confession didn't think that extramarital flirting (i.e. wanton looks, impudent or light behavior) was lawful. It is not addressed by name in the Bible, but it is addressed in principle in the seventh commandment. In *The Sufficiency of Scripture*, Noel Weeks takes great pains to lay the foundation for this use of Scripture:

> '[It is obvious] that the Bible's treatment of ethical or theological matters is not exhaustive in every detail. That raises a question. Even those who do not accept the authority of the Bible must concede that its authors intended it as a code for human conduct. How could it operate as such a code without being exhaustive? The raising of this question makes us ask how the Bible functions to direct conduct without being a multi-volume work covering every conceivable situation. It will also raise the question of whether we are right in expecting an authoritative source to say the last word on every detail of a subject.'[9]

---

8. Bolding mine.

9. Weeks, *The Sufficiency of Scripture*, p. 7.

> He goes on to say, '... one form an authoritative source could take is to cover every last detail of every aspect of the subject. That is the ideal to which some authors of definitive textbooks have aspired. There is another possible way. Seeking for exhaustive detail means a work so voluminous as to be practically impossible to produce or print. The other method chosen by those who have sought to say the last word on a subject has been to try to cover everything by means of a few general principles, rules, or laws. The belief then is that everything can be deduced once these general principles are understood. Thus the two possible approaches are at opposite extremes. One tries to state the case to the last minute detail. The other tries to sum up everything under a few general principles.'[10]
>
> '[T]he Bible,' Weeks continues, 'does not subscribe to either the approach of exhaustive detail or that of pure and general principles. The best example is the laws of Sinai and/or the laws recorded in Deuteronomy. Here we have an attempt to set forth rules to govern the community and personal life of Israel.
>
> 'The first impression of the Sinai and Deuteronomic covenants is of a mass of detail. Yet we also have general principles, the most obvious being the ten commandments....Thus Biblical legislation is not shaped by an abstract philosophical desire to reduce everything to a few general principles or to formulate a rule for every last detailed case. It is shaped much more by functional considerations. The general laws are clarified in matters of detail to avoid possible confusion.'[11]

Because of their generality, principles do not always have the obvious implications that commands do. Christians often differ on how to work them out in real life. The correct application

10. Weeks, *The Sufficiency of Scripture*, p. 8.

11. Ibid., pp. 8-10.

of biblical principles would be perfectly obvious to us in every situation if our minds were not clouded by sin, by worldly thinking, by preconceived ideas, by an unwillingness to see the truth. But because all of our minds are clouded to some degree by these hindrances, things do not look so clear cut, they often look gray. Because they are not obviously right or wrong, they have too often been called indifferent, but there is a very important distinction between the two. **Gray means that it is unclear *whether* it is black or white, bad or good. Indifferent means that it is *neither* black nor white, neither bad nor good.** We need to recognize gray areas as distinct from Christian liberty, because the doctrine of Christian liberty is designed to deal with things that are indifferent, that don't matter in and of themselves and don't affect the heart, but many gray areas are important, they do matter and do affect the heart.

Admittedly, many people misapply principles and come up with some wrongheaded ideas and try to force these ideas on others, but just because principles can be misapplied does not mean that they should not be correctly applied. Certainly it is easier, knowingly or unknowingly, to twist principles to support our preconceived ideas than it is to twist specific commandments (though plenty of people have managed this feat as well), but God has seen fit to give both general and specific instructions and faithfulness to His Word requires taking both seriously.

That people see the implications of biblical principles differently should be no surprise. It is also rare to find two people who agree completely on every single doctrine. The fact that people often come to different conclusions on what the Bible teaches does not mean that there are no right conclusions to come to; it does not mean that it is all relative, all personal, all subjective.

Herman Bavinck, arguably the greatest Dutch reformed theologian of his time, once said:

> '[T]he Bible is not the codification of laws, wherein we only have to look up article after article.... It is, therefore, the theologian's job to exegete Scripture meticulously and to cull out the truths that are deposited in the Word.... Reason, properly used, is both welcome and valued to elucidate the truths contained in Scripture, to compare biblical truth with biblical truth, and to deduce other truths from what God has revealed.'[12]

For example, nowhere in Scripture are we directly taught about the Trinity or that Jesus was 100 percent man and 100 percent God. These are doctrines which students of God's Word have deduced from other truths the Scriptures teach. Where the premises are sound and the reasoning is sound, the conclusions reached are also sound. The Bible wasn't given to us as a systematic theology textbook where we can look in the chapter on Christology to find out all about the nature of Jesus or the chapter on baptism to find out who should be its recipients. Neither was it given as a 'codification of laws, wherein we only have to look up article after article.' There is not a chapter on child rearing or a chapter on ethics in business or, for that matter, a chapter on modesty. Although there may be little to nothing said directly on such subjects, this doesn't mean there is not more that can be deduced from what is revealed.

For instance, have you ever realized that the Bible doesn't say a single thing about pornography? Yet, everyone realizes that

---

12. Herman Bavinck in a speech 'The Science of Holy Divinity' originally delivered in Dutch and later summarized in English by Ron Gleason in *Herman Bavinck: Pastor, Churchman, Statesman, and Theologian* (Phillipsburg, New Jersey: P&R Publishing Company, 2010), pp. 465-466.

pornography is a moral evil. Well, everyone but the 38 percent of adults and 5 percent of evangelical Christians, who, according to a 2003 Barna study[13], said that looking at pictures of nudity or sexually explicit behavior is morally acceptable. Barna predicts, furthermore, that these numbers will rise. They probably already have. How, then, can we say that pornography is wrong? We can do so by reasoning from what God's Word does reveal: that lust is wrong, that lust is often visually stimulated, and that public nudity is shameful. Do we say that pornography is a matter of Christian liberty just because the Bible never directly forbids it? No, a hundred times no!

What about child rearing? Besides giving a few general principles, there is not much the Bible spells out about how we should raise our children. Does this mean that child rearing is a matter of Christian liberty? That one method is just as good as another? That the parent who screams at his child to get him to do what he wants is just as right as the parent who speaks calmly and backs up his word with appropriate action not volume? There are no commands against screaming, after all. There are no commands about screaming, but there is a command about not provoking our children to wrath and there are commands about not giving vent to anger and from these we can deduce that we should not go around screaming at our kids. If it's not obvious to someone that viewing pornography or screaming at their kids is sinful, if their conscience is fine with it, that doesn't change the fact that it is still sinful. What would happen if we told people in these areas and in hundreds of others like them that they should just consult their own conscience, use it in moderation and be careful not to be a stumbling block to anyone, but that other than

13. The Barna Group www.barna.org. 'Morality Continues to Decay,' November 3, 2003 http://www.barna.org/barna-update/article/5-barna-update/129-morality-continues-to-decay. Used with permission.

that it was a matter of Christian liberty? I don't want to know! But, disturbingly, in many gray areas, this is exactly what they're being told.

C. Legalism: What It Is and What It Isn't

Because the matter of modesty has so often been abused by legalists (and, perhaps even more, because there is so much animosity towards the truth of modesty), it has become a touchy issue. Spinney writes: 'In many places today, to simply raise the subject of immodest clothing is to set off every legalism alarm in the building.'[14]

It is important to understand what legalism really is so that we do not make this charge falsely or retreat when we are charged falsely. In *The Grace of Law*, Ernest Kevan says that legalism is a term which is rarely used accurately. He goes on to try to set the record straight: '*The Oxford Dictionary* defines its theological meaning as "adherence to the Law as opposed to the Gospel; the doctrine of justification by works, or teaching which savors of it."'[15] Legalism, then, is first and foremost trying to earn salvation through works, and this is true even where these works are God's own commands. If you are trying to get to heaven by loving God with all your heart, mind and soul, you are a legalist. This legalism is probably far more prevalent than people think, because most Evangelicals know better than to say that they are trying to earn God's favor, but in their hearts they are living that way.

Legalism, then, is fundamentally a way of viewing the law; it is a heart disposition rather than an external mode of conduct. Legalism in regards to justification views the law as the means of earning one's salvation, but legalism can also be in regards to our view of sanctification. Kevan goes on to say: '... it is the use of the

---

14. Spinney, *Dressed to Kill*, pp. 2-3.

15. Ernest Kevan, *The Grace of Law: A Study in Puritan Theology* (Carey Kingsgate Press, 1964), p. 258.

Law "as pharisaically conceived"[16], and an employment of it in its outward form without regard to its inward demands."[17] So, then, legalism can also be focusing on the outward while ignoring the inward. If you are conscientious about dressing modestly, but allow pride and selfishness and anger to grow unchecked in your heart, then you are acting legalistically. This does not mean that you have to get your heart attitudes perfect before you can work on obeying the outward commands, but you do have to make sure you are always working on them together and never neglecting the inward man in order to polish up the outward man. God has made it clear that He takes no pleasure in whitewashed tombs and the same holds true for modest mummies. Both are full of dead men's bones!

Those who have a disproportionate focus on their own outward behavior will also tend to be those who put a disproportionate emphasis on the outward behavior of others. They will be quick to draw conclusions about people which are not warranted. However, contrary to popular belief, legalists aren't the only ones guilty of misjudging the heart based on outward practices. Those who rail the most against legalism are often those who see the demon of legalism lurking behind every long skirt and entrenched in every home without a TV and so are guilty of the very heart attitude they are so quick to condemn in others.

It is unfortunate that legalism has become associated with various standards and outward practices. It is true enough that all too often certain outward practices have been accompanied by an over emphasis on them to the point that they become the litmus test for true Christianity, but that is not always the case. Many of the heroes of the faith whom we all admire shared some of these same convictions. You cannot tell by the way a person

---

16. Here Kevan is quoting A.B. Bruce.

17. Ibid., p. 259.

dresses or by whether they have a TV or not or whether they dance or not, that a person is a legalist. **Legalism is not found in a particular set of standards; legalism is found in one's purpose for holding to those standards**. Is it being done to earn favor for salvation? Then it is legalism in regards to justification. Is it being done as a proof of one's holiness without due regard to the weightier matters of the law? Then it is also legalism, only this time in the area of sanctification. But if it is simply the outworking of one's conscience and one's understanding of biblical principles, then there is nothing the least bit legalistic about it.

Shades of legalism can also creep in by using general principles to make specific rules. Such rules may be useful, but once made are treated as absolute commands while forgetting the principles so that in abnormal situations where the principles would point to a different application, the rule is still enforced. I read the story once about a woman trying to make a recipe that had been passed down in her family for generations. She was puzzled by one particular step in the instructions and wondered why it was necessary, so she called her mom. Her mom had been doing it that way for years, but she also didn't know why it needed to be done that way. So she called the grandmother. The grandmother was sure it had to be done that way because it was the only way it had ever been done, but she also didn't know why. The great-grandmother was still alive so they went to ask her. It turned out that this step, which had been passed down for generations and considered indispensable, had to do with the open fire that the great-grandmother had been using to bake on and was rendered obsolete by the electric ovens that the last three generations had been using. This is an example of remembering the rule and forgetting the principle, so that rules are still followed even when there is no rationale for them.

Remember how we said earlier that it is wrong to scream at our children? Yet, is there never a time when it would be good and right to scream at them? What about if they are getting ready to walk in front of a car? Should you use your indoor voice to say: 'Honey, there's a car coming' and risk not being heard in time to prevent calamity? No, there is a time to yell. The principles governing modesty also can change based on the situation. If the house is on fire, you don't have to dress modestly before you flee. The Bible gives us a command not to murder and that includes not killing ourselves and when the house is burning down around you, a regard for the preciousness of life may cause you to come out less than fully dressed. Closer to everyday life, clothes which are modest on one body type may not be modest on a different body type. But although the standards of modesty will sometimes be applied differently, the standards themselves are the same and the different applications arise from objective realities, not subjective feelings.

Simon J. Kistemaker says it well when he says that we need to 'make a distinction between principle and application of that principle.'[18] A legalistic tendency results in forgetting the principles and remembering only the applications, the rules, and a refusal to acknowledge that extenuating circumstances may cause the principles to point to a different application. Any applications we come up with from general principles do not have authority on their own. Their authority is from the principles. If the principles don't apply in this case or if other principles override the application in this particular case, the application is no longer binding. This is part of the grayness of things not directly addressed in Scripture, but no matter how gray these questions may sometimes be, they are not things indifferent.

---

18. Simon J. Kistemaker, *New Testament Commentary: Exposition of the Epistles of Peter and of the Epistle of Jude* (Grand Rapids, MI: Baker Book House, 1987), p. 123.

My concern is that we will never take modesty as seriously as we should, we will never search out the principles which bear on it and never implement them conscientiously, as long as we believe that how we dress is a matter of Christian liberty, a thing indifferent. In the pages ahead we will continue our study of the general principles behind modesty, not to nail down the particulars once and for all, but so that each of us can make more biblically-informed decisions.

7: Three Principles of Modesty

Having seen that the Bible doesn't say that much directly about modesty but also having seen that that doesn't mean that nothing can be learned from what is said, let's look at three principles that together form much of the basis for understanding why immodesty is sinful.

A. It is wrong to lust

That is, it is wrong to desire to do what would be wrong to do or to desire to have what would be wrong to have. Josh Harris defines sexual lust this way: 'Lust is craving sexually what God has forbidden. To lust is to want what you don't have and weren't meant to have. Lust goes beyond attraction, an appreciation of beauty, or even a healthy desire for sex – it makes these desires more important than God. Lust wants to go outside God's guidelines to find satisfaction.'[1]

---

1. Josh Harris, *Sex Is Not the Problem (Lust Is): Sexual Purity in a Lust-Saturated World* (Colorado Springs, CO: Multnomah Books, 2003), pp. 20-21.

This principle of lust being wrong is found in many places in Scripture, here are a few as it relates to sexual lust:

> 'You have heard that it was said to those of old, "*You shall not commit adultery*." But I say to you that whoever looks at a woman to lust for her has already committed adultery with her in his heart.' (Matt. 5:27-28)

> 'Do not lust after her [the adulteress'] beauty in your heart, nor let her allure you with her eyelids.' (Prov. 6:25)

> 'Beloved, I beg you as sojourners and pilgrims, abstain from fleshly lusts which war against the soul…' (1 Pet. 2:11)

> 'For this is the will of God, your sanctification: that you should abstain from sexual immorality; that each of you should know how to possess his own vessel in sanctification and honor, not in passion of lust, like the Gentiles who do not know God; that no one should take advantage of and defraud his brother in this matter, because the Lord is the avenger of all such, as we also forewarned you and testified. For God did not call us to uncleanness, but in holiness.' (1 Thess. 4:3-7)

All Christians know that lust is wrong, but many don't realize how it operates and why it is so harmful. In his book, *Sex is Not the Problem (Lust Is)*, Josh Harris gets at the root of it: 'A man's lust leads him to detach a woman's body from her soul, mind, and person and use her for the sake of his selfish pleasure.'[2] This can be seen most dramatically at the far end of the continuum of lust where you have sadomasochism, a delight in causing pain which usually has a sexual element. This is where lust naturally leads, if you don't believe this, five minutes in a hard-core porn shop will convince you otherwise. There's a reason why handcuffs and rope can be found in such places. Even if

2. Harris, *Sex Is Not the Problem (Lust Is)*, p. 86.

it is just for playacting, it is an imitating of something wicked. Although, through the mercy of God, lust seldom goes that far, that is always what lust is at heart and we must not forget that. For this reason, lust must not be taken lightly; it must not be taken lightly by men giving way to their own lust and it must not be taken lightly by women encouraging, either purposefully or thoughtlessly, men to lust after them. Though few men go to the extreme of causing physical pain, leaving physical scars, hordes go far enough in their lust to cause much emotional pain, leaving emotional scars. Our sexuality was meant to be enjoyed holistically, with our whole souls and body being joined together, but lust is just interested in the body, creating a deformed and tragic expression of sexuality.

Abraham knew the power of lust, knew that it could even resort to murder to get its object and so asked his wife to lie, which seemed the lesser of two evils to him: 'And it came to pass, when he was close to entering Egypt, that he said to Sarai his wife, "Indeed I know that you are a woman of beautiful countenance. Therefore it will happen, when the Egyptians see you, that they will say, 'This is his wife'; and they will kill me, but they will let you live. Please say you are my sister, that it may be well with me for your sake, and that I may live because of you."' (Gen. 12:11-13). Verses 14-15 let us know that Abraham's fears were justified (though certainly not his method of self protection): 'So it was, when Abram came into Egypt, that the Egyptians saw the woman, that she was very beautiful. The princes of Pharaoh also saw her and commended her to Pharaoh.' Who Sarah is in relation to Abraham is probably one of the first questions the Egyptians ask and the thought in their minds seems to be, 'What do we have to do to get her for ourselves? If she's the wife, we'll have to do away with the husband, but if she's the sister we can just butter up the brother and she'll be ours.'

Lust wasn't just a problem for the pagan Egyptians, even the godliest of men struggled with it. David, a man after God's own heart, was conquered by it. 'Then it happened one evening that David arose from his bed and walked on the roof of the king's house. And from the roof he saw a woman bathing, and the woman was very beautiful to behold.... Then David sent messengers, and took her; and she came to him, and he lay with her...' (2 Sam. 11:2-4). It is sobering to realize that lust has been the downfall of the godly (David), the strong (Samson) and the wise (Solomon).

B. Temptations to lust are often visual

We will look at how this is especially true of men in the next chapter, but for now, let's look at a couple of verses:

> 'I have made a covenant with my **eyes**; Why then should I **look** upon a young woman?' (Job 31:1)

When Job commits to purity, when he commits to battling lust, he makes a covenant with his eyes. Not with his ears, not with his hands, not with his mouth. Temptation can come from many sources, but for men in particular lust often starts with the eyes.

> '...whoever **looks** at a woman to lust for her has already committed adultery with her in his heart.' (Matt. 5:28)

As well, visual stimulation was the point of entry for lust in the two instances we looked at in the last section, of the Egyptians with Sarah and of David with Bathsheba.

We have seen that the Bible teaches that lust is sinful, that men are particularly affected and that even godly men can be affected, and that lust often arrives through the eyes. But what does this have to do with immodesty?

C. IT IS WRONG TO TEMPT

If it were only wrong to lust, we would be off the hook in regards to the way we dress. But the Bible also teaches us that it is wrong to tempt. Many would like to think that it is solely the fault of the one lusting and that the source of the temptation doesn't bear any blame, but the Bible is very clear that if we do something to tempt someone to sin that that itself is sin: 'But whoever causes one of these little ones who believe in Me to sin, it would be better for him if a millstone were hung around his neck, and he were drowned in the depth of the sea. Woe to the world because of offenses! For offenses must come, but woe to that man by whom the offense comes!' (Matt. 18:6-7).

Closer to the topic at hand, Proverbs is full of warnings about the adulterous woman and how she tempts men with her eyes, with her words, with her body: Proverbs 5, 6:20-7:27, 9:13-18, 22:14, 23:26-28. Also, Numbers 25 and 31 chronicle the account of the Midianite women who tempted the men of Israel to sexual sin. In Numbers 31 Moses is furious that some of the Midianite women were left alive and he says, 'Look, these women caused the children of Israel, through the counsel of Balaam, to trespass against the Lord... now therefore, kill every male among the little ones, and kill every woman who has known a man intimately.' (Num.31:14-17).

Venning, in his book *The Sinfulness of Sin*, goes so far as to list tempting as one of those sins which are most like Satan.[3] This is not a sin to be taken lightly! If we tempt someone to sin then we are guilty of sin ourselves, *even* if the other person resists our temptation. The sin is in the tempting.

The examples in Proverbs and Numbers were of women tempting men to have sex with them. Maybe that seems far removed from the average Christian woman. She's not trying

---

3. Ralph Venning, *The Sinfulness of Sin* (Edinburgh: Banner of Truth Trust, 1993), p. 159

to get anyone to sleep with her; she just enjoys 'turning heads'. So the worst she might be responsible for is tempting a man to lust, that's not nearly the same thing as tempting someone to have sex. Or is it? The principle that Jesus reveals in Matthew goes both ways: if lusting after a woman is the same thing as committing adultery in your heart, then tempting someone to lust after you is the same thing as tempting someone to commit adultery. To put it another way, dressing in a way that says, 'Look at my body and drool' is the same heart attitude of Potiphar's wife who says, 'Lie with me' or the adulterous woman who says, 'Come, let us take our fill of love until morning.'

We have already seen that this correlation was not lost on the writers of the *Westminster Larger Catechism*. When they asked: What are the sins forbidden in the Seventh Commandment? (Thou shalt not commit adultery), they answered in part: immodest apparel (Question 139).

Robert Spinney, , in his book *Dressed to Kill: Thinking Biblically About Modest and Immodest Clothing*, says it well: 'If we wear clothing that encourages lust in someone else, then we are an accessory to lust. That makes us accessories to sin – regardless of our intentions.'[4] Notice the phrase 'regardless of our intentions.' Sometimes we think we are excused because we didn't intend to do harm, but if harm is caused by the careless choices we make, then we are responsible. It is like negligent manslaughter, the person may not have been intent on killing someone but their negligent actions led to someone dying and they are still blameworthy. Not, it is true, as blameworthy as if they had deliberately set out to do it, but still blameworthy.

The Puritan Richard Baxter says much the same thing in his *Christian Directory* in a section on clothing and how it can be used sinfully. Here is a paraphrase with the original in the footnotes:

4. Spinney, *Dressed to Kill*, p. 13.

'The outcome or effect of an action plays a large part in making it good or bad. Even if you did not intend to do harm, if you could foresee that harm was likely to come by your action, you will be sinning if you go ahead and do it anyway. For instance, if your clothing has the tendency to tempt those who see you to lust, even if that is not your intention, it is still your sin because you wore something which would probably result in their lust, yes, it is your sin if you did not do everything you could to avoid being a temptation. Although it is their sin that is ultimately the cause of lust, it is still your sin to be the unnecessary temptation. You must consider that you live among diseased souls! So you must not lay a stumbling block in their way or inflame the fire of their lust, nor allow your clothing to be a trap for them. Instead you must walk in a world full of sinners as you would walk holding a candle in a room full of gunpowder, or else you might not notice the fire which you refused to think about ahead of time and guard against, until it is too far gone to be put out. It is only a proud, impudent, lustful heart that wants so much to be admired and desired, that no fear of God, no fear of the sin and misery it will bring to them or others, can induce them to change the way they dress.'[5]

---

5. Richard Baxter in this excerpt is dealing with the question about whether we can use clothes to hide our deformity and make ourselves appear more beautiful than we really are. The original reads: 'Also the consequents concur much to make the action good or bad: though that be not your end, yet if you may foresee, that greater hurt than good will follow, or is like to follow, it will be your sin. As, (1.) If it tend to the insnaring of the minds of the beholders in procacious, lustful, wanton passions, though you say, you intend it not, it is your sin, that you do that which probably will procure it, yea, that you did not your best to avoid it. And though it be their sin and vanity that is the cause, it is nevertheless your sin to be the unnecessary occasion: for you must consider that you live among diseased souls! And you must not lay a stumblingblock in their way, nor blow up the fire of their lust, nor make your ornaments

Taking this seriously should cause us to be more careful in our choices. Too often we can have a flippant attitude that doesn't weigh our actions and decisions soberly enough. It's like being careless with our words and when people are hurt by something we said, we shrug it off saying we didn't mean to hurt them… and continue to say the same hurtful things! We have a responsibility to learn about the other gender and what is likely to tempt them and to do what we can to avoid it.

Robert Spinney also uses the qualifier 'encourages' ('If we wear clothing that *encourages* lust in someone else, then we are an accessory to lust') and this is an important clarification. A person does not share in the blame every time someone lusts after them, only when they have done something, whether purposefully or carelessly, to encourage, to tempt, another person to lust. People, especially the unconverted, have lust in their hearts and they are always looking for objects to lust after. A person may be dressed completely modestly and yet others will mentally undress them in order to lust after them. Sarah, wearing the robes of the times would have been dressed about as modestly as possible, but Abraham still knew that men would notice her beauty and would want her sexually. It is not wrong to be lusted after, it is wrong to *tempt,* to encourage, others to lust after us.

---

their snares; but you must walk among sinful persons, as you would do with a candle among straw or gunpowder; or else you may see the flame which you would not foresee, when it is too late to quench it. But a proud and procacious, lustful mind is so very willing to be loved, and thought highly of, and admired and desired, that no fear of God, or of the sin and misery of themselves or others, will satisfy them, or take them off.' – 'Christian Ethics' (chapter 10, part 3, question 3) in *The Practical Works of Richard Baxter*, p. 392.

8: Sexual Differences and Sin's Effect on Them

Modesty cannot be completely understood apart from sexuality[1]. It is not all there is to modesty, but there is a reason, as we saw in the second chapter, why modesty teaches us to cover our sexual organs and not our hands and feet and why small children often feel no embarrassment at running around naked but older, more sexually aware, children do. Modesty is tied up with our sexuality and the better we understand our sexuality, the better we will understand modesty.

When God made Adam, He saw that it was not good for Adam to be alone and so He made him a helpmeet to complement him. Adam was not complete and good in himself even when perfect; he was complete and good with Eve. What was true of Adam and Eve

1. Nor, according to Havelock Ellis, can sexuality be understood apart from modesty. On the first page of his multi-volume work *Psychology of Sex* he writes: 'It is necessary, before any psychology of sex can be arranged in order, to obtain a clear view of modesty.' He then spends fifty pages on the topic of modesty.

has been true of man and woman ever since. Woman complements man; woman completes man. This is true in many areas, it is true emotionally, mentally, physically and it is true sexually.

The fact that men and women are made for each other sexually means, first of all, that they are both sexual creatures with sexual appetites. Eve could not have completed Adam unless she too was sexual. Sometimes a man's sexuality is up-played and a woman's is downplayed. This may be because in the past Western culture has made it a virtue for women to be pure and innocent, which was interpreted as meaning not having those lower 'animal' instincts. It was assumed that sex was somehow base or evil, but this is not what the Bible teaches about sexuality. There is nothing incompatible about a woman being pure and sweet and also having sexual desires. God gave men and women both sexual urges and He called it good.

Another reason that women are sometimes thought not to be as sexual as men is because their sexuality is not necessarily displayed in the same ways or with the same intensity. Ethridge writes: 'When I hear people say that women don't struggle with sexual issues like men do, I cannot help but wonder what planet they are from or what rock they have been hiding under. Perhaps what they really mean is, the physical act of sex isn't an overwhelming temptation for women like it is for men.'[2]

Josh Harris talks about the misconceptions regarding the lusts of men and women:

> 'A major misconception about men is that their problem with lust is much worse and more serious than any woman's could be. In other words, that men are monsters while women are innocent and pure.'[3]

---

2 Ethridge, *Every Woman's Battle,* p. 13.

3. Harris, *Sex Is Not the Problem (Lust Is)*, p. 82.

> 'The truth is that men's lust is more obvious, but not necessarily more sinful. Guys are typically more visually orientated, and as a result their lust is more visible. And because God made men to initiate and pursue women, their expressions of lust are often more aggressive and blatant.'[4]

> 'When it comes to lust, the greatest misconception about women is that they only deal with lust on an emotional level. Over the years many Christian books (my own included) have emphasized that men struggle with physical desire and guarding their eyes, while women deal with their emotions. But if these generalizations aren't qualified, people might get the impression that women never struggle with lust as raw physical desire, or that their struggle against lust is less real.'[5]

Ethridge agrees:

> '... I have come to understand that in some way or another sexual and emotional integrity is a battle that every woman fights. However, many women are fighting this battle with their eyes closed because they don't believe they are even engaged in the battle. Many believe that just because they are not involved in a physical, sexual affair they don't have a problem with sexual and emotional integrity. As a result, they engage in thoughts and behaviors that compromise their integrity and rob them of true sexual and emotional fulfillment.'[6]

Understanding the nature of a woman's sexuality is fundamental to what is to come, because as long as men and women have their eyes closed in this battle with immodesty, we will never be able to conquer it. God made Eve the perfect helpmeet for Adam not by making her exactly like Adam, not by giving her the same

---

4. Harris, *Sex Is Not the Problem (Lust Is)*, p. 82.

5. Ibid., pp. 80-81.

6. Ethridge, *Every Woman's Battle*, p. 7

exact sexuality, but by giving her important differences which would complete and mesh with his own sexuality. As John Piper says, 'manhood and womanhood are to complement rather than duplicate each other.'[7]

The fact that we are incomplete without each other is most strikingly apparent sexually. Even anatomically it is self-evident that woman was made sexually for man. But these differences are far deeper than anatomical, a fact that many psychologists and feminists, after decades of denial, are being forced to realize:

> 'The 1960s and 70s saw an ideology that dismissed psychological sex differences as either mythical, or if real, nonessential – that is, not a reflection of any deep differences between the sexes *per se*, but a reflection of different cultural forces acting on the sexes. But the accumulation of evidence from independent laboratories over many decades persuades me that there are essential differences that need to be addressed. The old idea that these might be wholly cultural in origin is nowadays too simplistic.'[8]

One of the factors that accounts for these differences is varying levels of hormones. This started in the womb before society can be blamed for it. Doctor and psychiatrist Louann Brizendine describes it this way in her book *The Male Brain*: '... during weeks eight to eighteen [of pregnancy], testosterone from [a baby boy's] tiny testicles *masculinized* his body and brain, forming the brain circuits that control male behaviors.'[9]

---

7. John Piper, 'A Vision of Biblical Complementarity' in *Recovering Biblical Manhood and Womanhood: A Response to Evangelical Feminism,* ed. John Piper and Wayne Grudem (Wheaton, IL: Crossway Books, 1991), p. 49.

8. Simon Baron-Cohen, *The Essential Difference: The Truth about the Male and Female Brain* (New York: Basic Books, 2003), p. 10.

9. Louann Brizendine, *The Male Brain* (New York: Broadway Books, 2010), p. 12.

Gregg Johnson, professor of biology at Bethel College in St. Paul, writes in *Recovering Biblical Manhood and Womanhood* that this testosterone 'has an immediate effect on all of the organ systems, such that heart rate, respiratory rate, red blood cell counts, and brain structure are already sexually divergent at birth. The male testosterone level is two to three times that of the female until puberty, at which time it becomes, on the average, fifteen times higher than that of a female. Females produce about twice the estrogen of males prior to puberty and eight to ten times the estrogen after puberty.'[10]

Part of God knitting us together in our mother's womb was His using various hormones to change our bodies and our brains into either male or female. The varying proportions of testosterone and estrogen along with other chemicals such as vasopressin and oxytocin are responsible for many of the sexual and psychological differences between men and women.

But it's not all in the hormones. Doctor and psychologist Leonard Sax writes: 'In men, many areas of the brain are rich in proteins that are coded directly by the Y chromosome. Those proteins are absent in women's brain tissue. Conversely, women's brain tissue is rich in material coded directly by the X chromosome; these particular transcripts of the X chromosome are absent from men's brain tissue. These sex differences, then, are *genetically programmed*, not mediated by hormonal differences.... Scientists continue to recognize that sex hormones do affect the brain. However, this recent research has also demonstrated that the direct effect of the sex chromosomes on brain tissue need not be mediated by hormones. It's genetically programmed. It's present at birth.'[11]

---

10. Gregg Johnson, 'Biological Basis for Gender-Specific Behavior' in *Recovering Biblical Manhood and Womanhood*. Piper and Grudem, p. 284.

11. Leonard Sax, *Why Gender Matters: What Parents and Teachers Need to Know about the Emerging Science of Sex Differences* (Doubleday, 2005), pp. 14-15.

We often think of the differences between men and women in terms of strengths and weaknesses, but John Piper says it is more than that: 'God intends for all the "weaknesses" that are characteristically masculine to call forth and highlight woman's strengths. And God intends for all the "weaknesses" that are characteristically feminine to call forth and highlight man's strengths.... God intends them to be the perfect complement to each other, so that when life together is considered (and I don't just mean married life) the weaknesses of manhood are not weaknesses and the weaknesses of women are not weaknesses. They are the complements that call forth different strengths in each other.'[12] Linda Dillow and Lorraine Pintus put it this way: 'The differences He fashioned [between men and women] are an asset, not a liability[13].... Differences bring balance, fullness, and completion to a marriage.'[14]

Sex is about union, the union of man and woman. Two things that are exactly alike cannot have union in the way that two things that are different in a way designed to interlock with each other can. Think of two identical squares of cardboard. You can put them so close they are touching but they never become one, they cannot join together. Now think of two pieces of a puzzle, they are not exactly the same, but put them together and now you have one piece. The differences in the puzzle pieces allow them to have a greater union than they could if the pieces were all identical. In the same way, the sexual differences between men and women are designed to give them the highest union possible, such a union that the Bible describes it as a mystery and uses it as an illustration of the union we have in Christ.

---

12. Piper, 'A Vision of Biblical Complementarity' in *Recovering Biblical Manhood and Womanhood*, p. 49.

13. Dillow and Pintus, *Intimate Issues,* p. 35.

14. Ibid., p. 41.

A. MEN NORMALLY HAVE STRONGER SEXUAL DRIVES

Though men and women are both sexual creatures, men normally have stronger desires for intercourse. This difference is largely due to different levels of testosterone, which, as we saw in the last section, is about fifteen times higher in a boy at puberty than a girl. That translates into a much greater sexual drive. Dr. Brizendine gives a helpful way to picture this difference: 'Just as women have an eight-lane superhighway for processing emotion while men have a small country road, men have O'Hare Airport as a hub for processing thoughts about sex whereas women have the airfield nearby that lands small and private planes.'[15] This is not because men are beasts; it is how God has made them and it has a biological basis as well as, as with everything God does, a good purpose: if everyone had the sexual drive of the average woman, the human race may very well have become extinct by now!

God made men to be the stronger vessel and so they can better handle the stronger sexual drives. Sadly, because of sin, men often don't handle them well, but if you really wanted to see a perverse and decadent world, you should see a world where women were the ones with high levels of testosterone. How much reason we have to be thankful for God's wisdom in giving these necessary and purposeful desires to men more than to women. This is not to excuse the sin that comes when a man does not control his sexual drives, only to show that the strong sexual drives themselves are good and God-given.

This doesn't, however, mean that women never have strong desires for sex or that somehow it is unfeminine for them to do so. God did give sexual hormones to women as well and it is part of what He called good. Linda Dillow and Lorraine

---

15. Louann Brizendine, *The Female Brain*, (Morgan Road Books, 2006), p. 91.

Pintus describe it this way, 'A man is like a river. His testosterone levels flow constant and steady. A woman is like an ocean. Her hormones ebb and flow, depending on where she is in her menstrual cycle.'[16]

Nor does this mean that a woman can't or shouldn't have a stronger sexual drive than some men. What is true generally is not going to be true in every last instance. It is true, for example, that, *in general*, men are stronger physically than women, and yet, obviously, some women are stronger than some men. We recognize that a man isn't effeminate just because he isn't as strong as a particular woman and that a woman isn't unfeminine just because she is stronger than a particular man. This is also the case with the sexual drives of men and women. Some women will have stronger sexual drives than some men and there is nothing unfeminine about that.

B. Men are more stimulated by seeing and what they see and women are more stimulated by being seen and who sees them

This is part of how God has made men and women perfect for each other. Just like Jack Spratt and his wife got along so famously because he could eat no fat and she could eat no lean, so men and women are matched together wonderfully because men love to look at women and women love to be looked at by men.

Men love to look at women

It is no accident that pornography is usually geared to men while beauty products are usually geared to women. Marketers make it their business to know what people are like and what they want. Nor is it an accident that homosexual men are known for being

16. Dillow and Pintus, *Intimate Issues,* p. 37.

more clothes conscious and more fashion savvy than normal men. There are always dangers in generalizations, but on the whole women are far more concerned about their appearance than men[17]. As Josh Harris observes: 'He made men visually orientated, then made women beautiful.'[18]

We see this illustrated in the biblical examples we have already looked at concerning David and the Egyptians.

> David: 'And from the roof he **saw** a woman bathing, and the woman was **very beautiful to behold**.'

> Egyptians: '[Abraham thinking ahead says to Sarah:] I know that you are a woman of **beautiful countenance**. Therefore it will happen, when the Egyptians **see** you....' 'the Egyptians **beheld** the woman that she was **very fair**. The princes also of Pharaoh **saw** her.'

In both these cases, it wasn't when these men got to know Bathsheba and Sarah, it wasn't when they found out how funny or smart these women were, it was when they saw their beauty. We see this attraction to beauty evidenced in several examples of Scripture. It was an attraction to beautiful women that motivated the sons of God in Noah's day to take wives they

---

17. Fashion historians and psychologists try to say that this distinction is cultural and not generally true. Some of this is based on the fact that male birds are more brightly colored than female birds, some of it on the fact that at times in history it has been men who have dressed in ways that flaunt their bodies. While I don't have an explanation for why men have sometimes seemed to be the more appearance-conscious, I think the evidence is overwhelming that this is the exception and not the rule. Certainly the Bible's teaching assumes that men are more given to looking at women lustfully and women are more given to dressing inappropriately. Also, the teaching throughout church history indicates that these differences have held true for the last 2000 years.

18. Harris, *Sex Is Not the Problem (Lust Is)*, p. 85.

shouldn't have (Gen. 6:1-2). It seems to have been Rachel's beauty which attracted Jacob from the moment he laid eyes on her (Gen. 29:1-30). It was Esther's beauty that got her chosen as Queen (Esther 2:1-17). It was the former Queen's beauty that made her husband want to show her off as if she were a hunting trophy, placing her in a compromising situation (Esther 1:10-11). It seems to have been Tamar's beauty which was the main thing that attracted Amnon to her (2 Sam. 13:1).

Stephen Arterburn says in *Every Single Man's Battle*: 'As men we have an obvious vulnerability in our sexual makeup, and that's the ability of our eyes and our mind to draw vivid sexual gratification from the sensuality in the environment around us. To put it bluntly, our eyes and mind are capable of intense foreplay.'[19]

This was why when a king had a harem of beautiful women and needed someone to watch over them he relied on eunuchs. Normal men simply can't live in close proximity with beautiful women without being sexually attracted to them. And this is actually a good thing. The ability to receive pleasure through sight is a gift and it is part of what makes marriage so wonderful. This aspect of maleness is not a problem, it's a blessing. Some seem to think that men should be so godly as to be able to look on a woman revealing many of her charms without being affected. This is not to be godly, this is to be unmanly. This is to be emasculated. A godly man can and should resist the temptation to lust – resist looking at what he shouldn't see and resist thinking about what he shouldn't have seen – but not to notice women at all, not to be attracted by female beauty, not to enjoy looking, is against the masculinity God gave him.

This is not to say that men only are aroused by what they see, and women never are, but that men are more easily and intensely

19. Arterburn, Stoeker and Yorkey, *Every Single Man's Battle*, p. 11.

aroused in this way. As Kay Arthur, speaking for men and women, says: '...the mind is the most powerful sex organ in our bodies – and...the eyes serve as a catalyst to turn on the mind.'[20]

An important thing to observe about this catalyst is that our eyes don't find sexual stimulation exclusively by seeing sexual organs. Our society believes that it is okay to show cleavage as long as you don't show nipples and okay to show thighs as long as you don't show pudenda. Yet that such parts of the body are not the exclusive, maybe not even the primary, fuel for lust, is shown by the fact that hordes of men pore over the swimming suit edition of *Sports Illustrated* and yet few men, that I'm aware of, search medical textbooks for close-ups of sexual organs divorced from the rest of the body. It is the whole of the human form that is attractive and the more of that form that is shown the more attractive it is found. It is not, then, exclusively about *which parts* of the body are exposed, it is also about *how much* of the body is exposed. This is certainly not to say that all parts of the body are equally modest to show individually, but it is to say that we cannot boil modesty down to covering a few square inches of the body while the vast majority of it is left naked.

Women love to be looked at by men

Pastor John A. James writes, 'The propensity to personal decoration is, without all doubt, peculiarly strong in the female heart.'[21] I suppose this is universally acknowledged. But what is it that compels women to put so much thought in their appearance? God made woman for man, to sexually complement man and so women can receive a great deal of sexual pleasure through being seen, through feeling a man's eyes admiring their body.

---

20. Arthur, Kay, *Sex...According to God* (Colorado Springs, CO: WaterBrook Press, 2002), p. 192.

21. James, *Female Piety*, p. 221.

This is why parents often notice a huge difference in their daughters' concern for their appearance as they become teenagers. Girls, who a couple of years ago had cared very little about how they looked and who were happy to follow their parents' standards of modesty, now seem to spend half their time in front of the mirror and constantly test the limits of what they can wear. What has happened to these girls? Puberty and an awakening of their sexual desires.[22] As a girl's sexuality develops, she wants to be looked at. In the words of Dannah Gresh, they 'ache to be noticed and adored.'[23] There is nothing wrong with this desire, this ache, on the contrary, there is everything right with it, it is part of how God made women to complement men.

A psychologist writing on the differences between men and women writes: 'Women in conversation will often include personal reference to each other's appearance (their hair, their jewelry, their clothes) so as to praise the other's looks. It is astonishing how rapidly this will happen, often within seconds of first meeting. Let's say a husband and wife are visiting another couple. One of the women may open a conversation with her female friend by saying something like this: Oh, I love your dress. You must tell me where you got it. You look so pretty in it. It really goes well with your bag.'[24] He goes on to say how women will often go shopping together and consult one another about how this or that item of clothing looks on them. He then asks, 'When was the last time that you heard of two men going

---

22. Little girls also are generally more concerned about their appearance than little boys. Caring about appearance is not just a sexual trait that becomes evident at puberty; it is a feminine trait that is often evident very early on in childhood. However, it is one way a woman's sexuality is acted out and so often increases at puberty.

23. Gresh, *Secret Keeper,* p. 55.

24. Baron-Cohen, *The Essential Difference*, p. 50.

shopping together, getting into the same little booth, undressing in front of each other and asking each other whether this new shirt suited them?'[25] If you laughed at that thought then the truth of the sentiments is proved!

Women are particularly concerned with how they look to men they are interested in. An observant friend or mother can often tell when a woman is interested in a man by how she dresses around him. If a woman goes to a party with 100 people and ninety-nine of them tell her she looks beautiful, but the one man she was interested in doesn't seem to notice, the ninety-nine others aren't much of a consolation prize. Women do not get a thrill from being seen by men in general as much as they get a thrill when a man they find attractive notices them. Men are happy to look at any woman's body, but women tend to be more selective. In *Every Woman's Battle*, Ethridge gives several questions for married women to ask themselves in order to evaluate whether they are attracted to another man in an unhealthy way. One of these questions is, 'Do you select your daily attire based on whether you will see this person?'[26] A woman's sexual desires are often acted out through her dress.

Obviously these things are more true for some women [and men] than for others. Women are not cookie-cutter beings with cookie-cutter sexualities and neither are men. All women do not complement all men, men have different needs and women are also designed differently. But in general, to one degree or another, this is true of the man-woman relationship.

In the same way that our sexual differences allow us to have greater intimacy in a good way, so sin perverts our sexual differences to feed off one another in a bad way. Because men are

---

25. Baron-Cohen, *The Essential Difference*, p. 51.

26. Ethridge, *Every Woman's Battle*, p. 94.

stimulated by seeing and women are stimulated by being seen, sin causes men to want to see what they should not see and for women to show what they should not show:

> 'Men are tempted to give themselves to pornography – women are tempted to *commit* pornography.'[27] – Dr. Albert Mohler

> '…one way a woman acts out lust is to incite lust in men.'[28]
> – Josh Harris

A secular author puts it even more bluntly, 'seductive clothing is part of sexual foreplay.'[29] That is, immodest clothing can have the same effect of stirring up sexual desires on both the man *and the woman* as foreplay would, even though they haven't even touched. An example of this can be seen from an incident during the mid-Victorian era with its décolletages which left little to the imagination and which caused 'excitement in both wearer and viewer…. A young lady of that time described the frisson of going to the theatre for the first night of an opera by Offenbach, and how hard it was to work out which was the more stimulating – the music, or the sensation of being half-naked in close proximity to a male.'[30]

And just to show that this is no new phenomenon, here is a quote taken from the second century A.D.: 'On no account must a woman be permitted to show to a man any portion of her body naked, for fear lest both fall: the one by gazing eagerly, the

---

27. Albert Mohler, quoted in Josh Harris, *Sex Is Not the Problem (Lust Is)*, p. 87.

28. Harris, *Sex Is Not the Problem (Lust Is)*, p. 88.

29. Ruth P. Rubinstein, *Dress Codes: Meanings and Messages in American Culture* (Westview Press, 2001), p. 135.

30. Prudence Glynn, *Skin to Skin: Eroticism in Dress* (London: Book Club Associates, 1982), p. 52.

other by delighting to attract those eager glances.'[31] – Clement of Alexandria.

Women want to believe that they are just trying to look pretty and can't help it that men have a problem with it. But in reality it's the very fact that men are turned on by seeing a woman's body that makes them want to show their bodies. It is not an innocent desire that just happens to be harmful for men. If men were turned on by the sight of a woman in green gloves, women would want to wear green gloves.[32] *Immodest dress does not just provoke lust in men, it feeds lust in women.* Putting on an outfit that shows her body off to good advantage gives a woman a bit of a high, having an attractive man take a second glance at her gives her a real high. These desires are not wrong when in their proper place, in marriage, with her husband, but when a woman begins to seek other men's admiring glances, then she is just as surely sinning as the man who gazes sensually at women other than his wife. And, in both cases, feeding lust has the same result: the desire for what one shouldn't have grows.

This is not to say that every woman who dresses immodestly is deliberately trying to get a man to lust after her body. There

---

31. Clement of Alexandria, *The Instructor*, book 2, chapter 2 quoted in Havelock Ellis, *Studies in the Psychology of Sex:Volume 1* (Philadelphia: F.A. Davis Company, 1910), p. 27.

32. The psychologist J. C. Flügel has a thought-provoking answer to the objection that men shouldn't be so easily aroused and so the problem of lust is all the man's problem and women bear no responsibility. He admits that there is truth in that 'it correctly diagnoses the presence of masculine desire,' but goes on to say that this argument also 'incorrectly endeavors to hide the presence of a corresponding feminine wish to excite and "play up" to this desire.' He concludes by saying that 'women endeavor to project their own guilt onto men, in much the same way as men have, in the past, projected theirs on to women.' –*The Psychology of Clothes* (International University Press, 1969), p. 110.

is a continuum of awareness among women about what they are doing[33]. A few are completely aware and a few are completely unaware, but most Christian women fall someplace in the middle. Women were made for men and part of that means that they innately have a pretty good idea of what will turn a man's head. However, this desire to turn heads can easily fly under the radar because it isn't usually accompanied by a desire for sex itself. Women are not as tempted as men to go 'all the way' and so it is easier to be unaware of the sexual nature of their desires to attract a man's admiring glance[34]. They have some idea, there are some whispers from their conscience and their experience that there is something wrong, but it is so easy to ignore these whispers because they like the feeling they get when they dress a certain way and because everyone else is doing it. They aren't deliberately and purposefully trying to seduce men, but are in denial of why they are doing what they are doing. They often give it a more acceptable name and say something like, 'I just want guys to notice me' or 'It's just nice to know I'm still attractive.' Like parents who smile and say their out of control child is

---

33. Men often go through stages about where they think women are on this continuum. When they are single they tend to think women are consciously trying to seduce them or at least tantalize them. The effect of immodesty is so apparent to them that they can't believe that the woman is not equally conscious of it. When they get married, they slowly learn that women are not as deliberate as they had thought. When their own daughters reach puberty and start testing the limits of what they can wear, they have a hard time imagining that any sexual intent is involved.

34. Though there is much I disagree with Flügel on, I do find some of his observations thought provoking. In *The Psychology of Clothes*, he says that because a woman's sexuality is more diffuse, it is more easily able to escape recognition as such and the woman herself may not be aware of these motives. He says, 'in witnessing female exposure, man is often more acutely conscious than woman herself of its sexual intention.' – p. 108

enthusiastic, it is not a conscious piece of misinformation; they just don't want to admit that things are as bad as they really are.

But we can only deal with sin when we see it for what it is. In order to stop feeding and start fighting lust, women need to be honest with themselves about what they're dealing with. Part of the difficulty of being honest is that there is often an unhealthy expectation for women not to have overtly sexual desires and so they can be afraid that if they own up to it they will be met with shock and disgust, whereas men, even very godly men, can admit to struggling with lust and no one thinks anything about it, perhaps they are even commended for their honesty. A woman's longing to be seen and to attract is in itself a good desire, the goal should not be to stigmatize it, deny that it's there or kill it, but to keep it from being channeled in wrong ways. We looked at this in our chapter on modesty and beauty when we saw how important it is for a woman to be content to be beautiful to *one* man.

This difference between men and women is especially fundamental to modesty and we will come back to it again and again.

C. Men are more stimulated by initiating, women are more stimulated by responding

As Josh Harris puts it: 'A man is created to pursue and finds even the pursuit stimulating;[35] a woman is made to want to be pursued and finds even being pursued stimulating.'[36] We can only marvel at God's goodness in thinking of details like this. If both men and women wanted to be the pursuers, or if they both wanted to be

35. John Piper agrees: 'Mature masculinity expresses its leadership in romantic sexual relations by communicating an aura of strong and tender pursuit.' 'A Vision of Biblical Complementarity' in *Recovering Biblical Manhood and Womanhood: A Response to Evangelical Feminism,* ed. John Piper and Wayne Grudem (Wheaton, IL: Crossway Books, 1991), p. 40.

36. Harris, *Sex Is Not the Problem (Lust Is)*, p. 85.

the pursued, it would be hard to have a fulfilling relationship. But when one delights in responding, in being sought out, in being noticed, in being desired, and the other delights in initiating, seeking, noticing, desiring, then it is truly a match made in heaven.

This aspect of the male and female relationship is part of how marriage pictures the relationship of God with His bride, the church. God was the initiator, He sought us when we weren't seeking Him, we love Him only because He first loved us.[37] As the hymn says:

> 'From heaven He came and sought her
> To be His holy bride;
> With His own blood He bought her
> And for her life He died.'[38]

In light of this, it is noteworthy that in many 'how we met stories' it was the man who started pursuing the woman before the woman had taken much notice of him.

God appears to have again used biological means to work out this difference. Dr. Leonard Sax writes, 'The neurochemical basis for both love and sex in females involves the hormone oxytocin, the same hormone released when a mother breast-feeds her newborn baby.... In males on the other hand the hormone underlying sexual attraction is not oxytocin but testosterone, the same hormone that mediates the aggressive drive.'[39]

Dr. Gregg Johnson writes, 'Predatory aggression is stimulated by centers in the amygdala. Males tend to have a larger amygdala and have more neural connections between the amygdala and other centers of aggression in the hypothalamus....it is known

---

37. 1 John 4:19

38. Samuel J. Stone, 'The Church's One Foundation' (1866).

39. Sax, *Why Gender Matters,* p. 122.

that men have significantly larger preoptic areas and amygdalae than women, and it may be reasonable to assume that the cause of differences in human aggression do have a biological basis.'[40]

Men were made to be more aggressive, to love a challenge, to not be so afraid of being hurt, to be willing to take risks and go after what they want. This is not to say that women cannot be like this or should not be like this in some ways, only that in general men are, in good and bad ways, more aggressive.

Women were made to be less aggressive, they long to be sought after and pursued. Because a woman has these longings, it can be hard to go month after month and year after year with no man noticing her, showing interest in her, with no man pursuing her. This desire itself is not wrong, it is good, but what will a woman do with that desire? Will she submit to God's plan for her life at that time, trusting Him to meet her needs, and accept that no one is pursuing her and that she can be happy without that? Or will she, by various means, including dressing to attract attention, see what she can do to get a man to pursue her? If not pursue her in marriage, at least pursue her in his mind and heart? For a woman seduction does not have to mean getting a man into bed with her, seduction can just mean getting into his heart, knowing that his heart races a little when she is around him.

Josh Harris talks about how these things are twisted by sin: 'Lust blurs and bends true masculinity and femininity in harmful ways. It makes a man's good desire to pursue all about "capturing" and "using," and a woman's good desire to be beautiful all about "seduction" and "manipulation".'[41]

---

40. Johnson, 'Biological Basis for Gender-Specific Behavior' in *Recovering Biblical Manhood and Womanhood*, p. 286.

41 Harris, *Sex Is Not the Problem (Lust Is)*, p. 86.

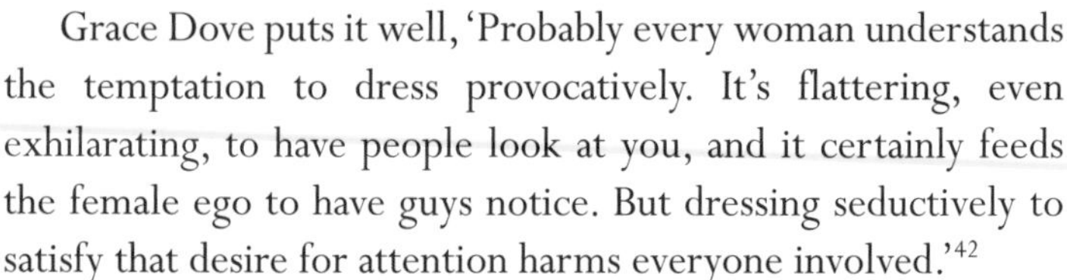

Grace Dove puts it well, 'Probably every woman understands the temptation to dress provocatively. It's flattering, even exhilarating, to have people look at you, and it certainly feeds the female ego to have guys notice. But dressing seductively to satisfy that desire for attention harms everyone involved.'[42]

D. Men can be aroused instantaneously, women normally become aroused over time

As someone has put it so succinctly: 'Men are microwaves, women are crockpots.' This tendency of men to be quickly aroused is often thought of as a bad thing, but, in and of itself, it is a good thing, with a good purpose. The fact that men are so quickly aroused is one of the things that makes them the initiators in relationships. If men and women were both slowly aroused and had to spend a lot of time with each other before they became interested, there would be much less opportunity for attachments to form. Again, how many 'how we met stories' involve the man knowing right away she was the one for him and wooing the woman until she returned his love? This is probably also part of the reason that arranged marriages were able to work in situations where the bride and groom didn't know each other beforehand. If men and women were both slowly aroused, it would be a long, cold honeymoon! But when one can be immediately attracted to the other and delight in seeking to win the heart of the other, and when the other can be flattered at the attention and enjoy being slowly won over, then it may actually work quite well.[43]

42. Grace Dove, *Secrets about Guys (that shouldn't be secret)* (Standard Publishing, 2005), p. 21.

43. This is not said in order to promote arranged marriages, nor to say that they always work out this way, only to explain how they can and have worked sometimes.

Dr. Gregg Johnson explains the biology behind this difference: 'The thresholds to set off responses in the limbic system differ between males and females. In males, testosterone stimulates the production of neurotransmitters in the hypothalamic area. This excess of neurotransmitters waiting in readiness in the synaptic areas tends to lower the threshold of response in males, such that less stimulation is required to set off behavioral responses to such things as food, sexual, or threat stimuli. Elevated estrogen in females has the opposite effect, inhibiting synaptic firings in the brain region and requiring more sensory and cognitive stimulation in order to elicit the same response.... These differences may explain the gender-specific reactions of males and females in sexual interactions.'[44]

Women can and do lust, but when they do it is usually not so quickly aroused. We can see this by comparing two examples of lust in the Bible. Let's start with women, the crockpots: '...Now Joseph was handsome in form and appearance. And it came to pass after these things that his master's wife cast longing eyes on Joseph, and she said, "Lie with me."' (Gen. 39:6-7). In the case of Potipher's wife, it appears that she had been around him for sometime. He had had time to show himself a faithful servant, time for Potipher to realize that God's blessing is on him because of Joseph and time for him to make Joseph overseer of all his house. The Bible says, 'and it came to pass *after these things* that his master's wife casts longing eyes on Joseph.'

Compare Potipher's wife the crockpot with David the microwave: 'Then it happened one evening that David arose from his bed and walked on the roof of the king's house. And from the roof he saw a woman bathing, and the woman was very beautiful

44. Johnson, 'Biological Basis for Gender-Specific Behavior' in *Recovering Biblical Manhood and Womanhood*, p. 286.

to behold.... Then David sent messengers, and took her; and she came to him, and he lay with her...' (2 Sam. 11:2-4). This wasn't something that built up over time. The first time he saw her naked in her bathtub he ended up with her naked in his bed.

That men are more quickly triggered to lust is also one of the reasons prostitutes are more likely to be women. A woman can stand on a street corner showing off her body and can pick up men just as they are passing by. They see, they lust and they are ready to do business. It doesn't take much and it doesn't take long. This is also why the book of Proverbs is filled with warnings to men of the adulterous woman who will stand in the streets seeking to allure them. For a woman, it will usually take a lot more than a man standing on a street corner showing his legs to get her in bed with him. If a man wants to entice a woman into bed with him he usually has to first get her heart and that takes time.

Shaunti Feldhahn tells a story in her book *For Women Only: what you need to know about the inner lives of men* that demonstrates how quickly men can be aroused. She describes this man as a 'faithful husband whom I highly trust' and goes on to share his admission: 'If I see a woman with a great body walk into Home Depot and I close my eyes or turn away until she passes, for the next half hour I'm keenly aware that she's in there somewhere. I'm ashamed to say that, more than once, I've gone looking down the aisles, hoping to catch a glimpse.'[45] Even more catastrophically, Stephen Arterburn, the author of *Every Man's Battle* confesses to driving his Mercedes into the back of a Chevelle because his eyes were captivated by a beautiful and scantily dressed jogger on the side of the road.[46]

---

45. Shaunti Feldhahn, *For Women Only: What You Need to Know about the Inner Lives of Men* (Multnomah, 2004), p. 113.

46. Arterburn, Stoeker and Yorkey, *Every Man's Battle*, pp. 9-10.

When women hear stories like these, which are often so foreign to their own experience, they often dismiss such men as being sick or having problems. There is a sense in which that is true, men are sick and do have problems, it's called sin and it affects all of us, just in different ways. Feldhahn goes on to say, 'I'd love to think that this man was an aberration – except that all the men I shared his quote with said, "That's *exactly* right!"' When men share their struggles with lust and feel like they are viewed as monsters for having these struggles, they become less likely to open up which creates a cycle where women understand even less about how men are wired. As difficult and even upsetting as it can be for a woman to understand and accept the flammable nature of a man's sexual drive, it is important for several reasons:

- It helps her take it seriously and not trifle with it, not trifle with it through her clothes, not trifle with it through leaving lingerie catalogs around, not trifle with it by 'playing' with men in a flirtatious way, thinking that she won't let it go too far, with no idea that she is playing with fire.

- It teaches a woman not to blame herself for her husband's wandering sexual appetite, thinking that it must be because she is not attractive enough or loving enough. As the authors of *Every Man's Battle* say, 'If a husband has a problem with his eyes, his wife often puts useless pressure on herself to improve her looks or to go out of her way to do nice things for him, thinking it will solve the problem.... But if a man has eye problems, it *isn't* because his wife needs to look more enticing.'[47]

- It keeps a woman from overreacting, from responding with undue abhorrence, finding it impossible to respect

47. Arterburn, Stoeker and Yorkey, *Every Man's Battle: Winning the War on Sexual Temptation One Victory at a Time*, pp. 147-148.

> and admire the godly men in her life when she learns of their struggles.

Two things must be clarified. In saying that God made men to be more quickly aroused, we must not excuse men when their God-given drives are perverted by sin. Though men have unique temptations, God gives grace to all of us, whatever the temptations are in our lives, to live pure and holy lives. To excuse our sin – or the sin of others – because of how God made us is to accuse God of sin. Second, in saying that these things are particularly true of men, we must not think that these things are never true of women or that something is wrong with them when they are. God has made us all different and there is beauty in our variety.

These four points of difference are important to bring out because so many women seem to resent having to adapt their dress to the weaknesses of men, and the huge sacrifice this is, not realizing that their own sin is just as great as the man's and is very often what makes them want to wear such clothes. Lust is a sin men and women share in equally. Just because a woman can more easily walk away from it without going all the way does not mean she is any the less guilty. Dressing modestly is not a matter of curtailing our liberty to avoid being a stumbling block to our weaker brother, we do not have the liberty to feed our own lust or own ego by inciting lust in men.

Josh Harris puts it perfectly, 'Lust seeks to use what we know about the weaknesses of the opposite sex to manipulate them. Isn't it wonderful that as brothers and sisters in Christ we can use this same information to help each other pursue holiness?'[48]

---

48. Harris, *Sex Is Not the Problem (Lust Is)*, p. 94.

E. THE STRENGTH OF IMMODESTY

1. Immodesty is a sexual sin

If it were simple ignorance, it would be enough to tell a woman not to wear such and such and that would be the end of the problem (and in a few cases, that is enough to solve the problem, but in many more it is not). If it were simply that it is so hard to find modest clothes, it would be enough to start a store that sells modest clothes and that would be the end of the problem. But experience teaches us that it is not usually so simple. The battle is hard, in part, because sexual desires are strong and do not die easily.

2. Immodesty is a natural sin

Sometimes we think that it is only because our culture is so sensual that Christian women are prone to dress immodestly, but there are other things about our culture that are equally strong and yet are not so compellingly influential. Our culture has, in the past especially, taught that it is degrading for a woman to stay at home and care for her children, but there is something inherent in the heart of a mother that wants to be with her children and so it does not require too much persuasion to convince a woman to stay at home whenever possible. It is where her heart is anyway. But we cannot expect the battle over immodesty to be won so easily. When fighting immodesty, we are fighting against something ingrained in a woman's very nature, not just something urged on her by the outside forces of her culture. Modesty is hard because modesty requires dying to self.

3. Immodesty is a feminine sin[49]

When I was researching this book, I was surprised by how much was written on modesty by feminists and how they (especially

49. This is certainly not to say that men cannot and do not sin in this way. Men are sometimes guilty of immodesty. However, men are not normally as tempted in this way. Men and women both have temptations that they are particularly prone to because of their gender.

old-school feminists) often railed more strongly than anyone against immodesty. I finally realized that feminists, in rejecting everything feminine, also rejected feminine sins. It's not the sinfulness of it that bothers them; it's the femininity of it. Feminists are for 'modesty' because to dress to attract is part of feminine nature. The desire to have a man appreciate her body is every bit as basic to a woman's femininity as the desire to have a child or to have someone to look out for and protect her and though those desires are not sinful, they can easily lead to sin. Modesty is not just 'for the guys' to help them overcome sin; it is about overcoming a woman's sin too.

4. Immodesty is a self-deceived sin

Have you ever been around someone who was very sure they were humble but who made it obvious to all around them that they were proud? Their pride colored their thinking so that they thought their prideful speech sounded humble, that their prideful actions looked humble. They weren't aware of being proud, they were self-deceived. Or have you ever noticed someone who thought of themselves as selfless but who managed in their 'selflessness' to manipulate others into doing what they wanted to do? Again, their selfishness prevented them from seeing what people really needed and wanted and instead they projected their own needs and wants onto them. This is the way of sin and this is the way of immodesty. Few Christian women purposefully and consciously dress immodestly, but often their native bent to sensuality blinds them to the immodesty of their clothing.

This is not to say that people never dress immodestly with a pure heart. It does happen, just like sometimes people say something that sounds proud even though they really are humble or do something that looks selfish even though they really are selfless. But it is to say that, more often than not, people are self-deceived about their motives and desires. This should make us circumspect in watching over our own hearts and the hearts of those we are responsible for, especially our wives and daughters. Realize that sensuality may be what makes it so hard to get the lesson of modesty through to your wife or daughter. It's not necessarily just an innocent lack of understanding. This makes it all the more important that you not give up, you are not just fighting for their clothes, you are fighting for their hearts; you are not just fighting to protect the eyes of the men around them, you are fighting to protect them from the lust that is in their own hearts.

5. *Understanding the battle*

We must understand the battle we are in if we are to fight it effectively. All too often we step into the ring with immodesty and expect that a few words about how such-and-such clothes are detrimental to men will be enough to knock immodesty down for the count. We too often have underestimated our opponent and stand bewildered when our words bounce off him without even causing him to blink. I have heard immodesty addressed on numerous occasions but it seems to be the normal experience that nothing changes. Why is this? There may be many answers, but I think one of the problems is that we don't know what we are up against. The first step is seeing immodesty for what it is: a sexually-motivated sin inherent in the very nature of a woman.

F. SOME BALANCING THOUGHTS

It needs to be made clear that though these things are often true of a woman to some degree, they are not true of every last woman and they are certainly not true to the same degree in every woman. Women are different. Not all of them love to shop, talk on the phone, eat chocolate and have pedicures. There are women who are not particularly tempted to catch another man's eye by their dress. We all have different temptations and areas of weakness. Though this area of weakness is one that is too often overlooked, we need to be careful not to go to the opposite extreme and see it where it does not exist.

When we see a woman dressing immodestly, we should not assume that she has sexual intent. The sexual fulfillment that comes from dressing immodestly comes when a woman has some inkling or another that what she is wearing will have an effect on men. But immodesty is so prevalent in our culture that a woman may wear revealing clothing without thinking anything about it.

We also have to keep in mind that people have different standards of modesty and they may sincerely be striving to dress modestly, desiring to protect the men around them and to keep their own hearts from impurity, but see the issue of modesty differently than we do and come to different conclusions. We've already made the point, and we're going to make it again, that the standards of modesty don't change, but we've also made the point that the standards of modesty are not crystal clear and so we're never all going to be on the same page. This chapter's thoughts about the sexuality of immodesty are written primarily for us to examine our own hearts and to shed light on how to deal with those we are responsible for, our daughters, our wives, and, secondarily to give us insight into the problem of immodesty as a whole. They are not meant for us to make assumptions based only on what we see of a person's clothes.

9: Modesty and Sexuality

A. Modesty and the Mind

As Linda Dillow and Lorraine Pintus write in their book *Intimate Issues: 21 Questions Christian Women Ask About Sex*, '…the mind is the most important sexual organ….The mind is the command center for all sexual feelings. It's the congress that governs your sexual state.'[1] Because this is so, what we put into our minds has a great potential to influence us sexually. This section will focus on concerns that relate especially to women, though they have application to men, because these things more directly affect the subject of this book.

In her book *Every Woman's Battle*, Shannon Ethridge devotes a whole chapter to the mind and the role it plays in our sexual integrity. The title to one of the sections in that chapter is a truth we all need to take to heart: **Thinking Equals Rehearsing**. We all too often think our thoughts are relatively harmless and

1. Dillow and Pintus, *Intimate Issues,* p. 23.

don't really affect anything. Ethridge does an excellent job of bashing that myth:

> 'Imagine an actor preparing to perform in a play. She memorizes her lines, gets inside the character's head, and tries to imagine how this person would feel and act. She rehearses being the person. She thinks intently about doing what that person would do and saying what that person would say exactly the way she would say it. The more she's rehearsed being that character, the sharper and more "automatic" her performance.
>
> 'Something similar happens when we fantasize sexually or emotionally about inappropriate or sinful behavior. We are rehearsing when we think about the conversations we would have with a particular man if we were ever alone with him, when we entertain thoughts of an intimate rendezvous, or wish that a certain man would take special notice of us. When we rehearse these scenarios, we imagine what we will say and do in these encounters. Then when Satan lays the trap and leads that man in your direction, guess what? We are more than likely going to play the part exactly the way we have rehearsed it.'[2]

It is not enough to dress modestly if we allow ourselves to think immodestly. We can sin sexually with nothing but our minds. This is what Jesus was saying when He said that a man who lusts after a woman has committed adultery with her already in his heart. Likewise, and listen to this carefully, *when a woman imagines dressing immodestly and about men checking her out, she has already committed adultery with these men in her heart.* I suppose we all know that men can be turned on by imagining seeing a scantily-dressed woman, but what many don't realize is that women can be turned on by imagining being seen while scantily-dressed – and that they do this more than they or we might like to think. This is an area

2. Ethridge, *Every Woman's Battle*, p. 74.

I have not always been as thoughtful about as I should have been. I was a teenager when I first began taking modesty seriously and since then I don't know if I have ever gone out in public wearing anything I believed to be immodest, but I have too often thought about what it would be like to wear something immodest and the attention I would get. I thought it wasn't that bad since I wasn't actually doing it. But by such imaginations I was, as Etheridge put it, rehearsing immodesty. I am thankful that in God's grace those rehearsals never culminated in a performance, but those rehearsals were sinful in and of themselves and they could so easily have led to even greater sin.

In the same chapter on the mind, Shannon Ethridge gives a list of personal convictions that help her guard her mind. I will quote one because I think it is an area we often don't think about when we think about guarding our minds:

> 'I choose not to read romance novels. I consider steamy romance novels to be pornography for females. (The sexually graphic pictures are mental rather than visual, which is more alluring to women.) They often glamorize sex outside of marriage and can arouse us sexually. I am also careful about Christian romance novels if I find myself comparing my husband to the hero in the story and thinking about all the ways Greg [author's note: Greg is her husband] doesn't measure up. I want to protect my marriage by resisting any thoughts that may evoke feelings of disillusionment and disappointment with reality.'[3]

I also stopped reading such books, whether it was one of the Christian romance novels that 'everyone says is harmless' or whether it was one of the classic love stories that 'everyone should read,' for similar reasons. Too often we evaluate books and movies in the light of what is blatant. Are there detailed descriptions

---

3. Ethridge, *Every Woman's Battle*, pp. 76-77.

of sexual acts? Are the characters engaging in sex outside of marriage? and so on. If it passes these tests, we figure it is good, clean entertainment. We fail to see that continually putting before our minds men that are handsome and charming and near perfect creates unhealthy expectations in us of what the husband we have now should be or of what the husband we will have one day will be. This is one way romance novels are like pornography: they both create expectations for things that are unattainable in real life so that we are not as able to enjoy what real life has to offer. The result is that just as many women choose a fantasy romantic life over a real romantic life as men choose a fantasy sex life over a real sex life.

The other danger of romance novels is that they often portray romance as the main source of happiness and fulfillment for their character. However, in real life, romance is not something that can fill all the emotional needs of a woman. She needs a variety of relationships and activities and especially a close relationship with God to be happy. Romance novels, however, can give the impression that romance is all there is to life and if you have that you have everything and if you don't have that you have nothing. They can also give the idea that a relationship with a man is all about romance. Again these things mirror pornography, which gives the idea that life is all about sex and especially that a relationship with a woman is all about sex. Both are damaging to a happy marriage in real life, to a happy romance and to a happy sex life. This does not mean that every book which contains elements of romance is dangerous for that would include biographies of some very godly men and women! It is the perspective on, not the presence of, romance that is important to consider.

We should also be careful of the thoughts about sexuality that we put into our children's minds through the cartoons that they watch. Many of the newer cartoons are filled with sexual innuendos, sensual dress and behavior and unhealthy relationships between men and women. But even older cartoons are guilty. Evidently they thought they could get away with sensuality if they portrayed it between two animals. So you have the female dog (or cat or, more recently, a car or a toy) strutting her stuff, batting her eyes, swaying her hips and you have the male dog panting after her. This is not how a godly woman should try to get the attention of a man and it is not the attention a godly man should give to a woman not his wife. Let's be careful about putting this before our children's eyes, influencing what they see as normal and permissible attitudes between men and women.

B. A Bodyguard Named Modesty

Josh Harris says it so well, 'Yes, lust is bad. But it's bad because what it perverts is so good….We need to keep reminding ourselves that our goal is to rescue our sexuality from lust so we can experience it the way God intended.'[4]

I have read dozens of books on the subject of clothes written by sociologists, psychologists, sexologists, feminists, fashion historians and more and almost every single one has made fun of the church leaders throughout the centuries who have condemned immodesty. These authors have laughed at their naivety in promoting modesty since modesty in the end only encourages sexuality. What these sociologists, psychologists, sexologists, feminists and fashion historians don't know is that Christians don't want to destroy sexuality, they want to protect it. God has given us laws for our good and this includes the laws governing our sexuality. He is the One who created us as sexual beings and the purpose of His laws is not to destroy our sexuality, but to make us as sexually whole and fulfilled as possible in a fallen world.

---

4. Harris, *Sex Is Not the Problem (Lust Is)*, pp. 11-12.

It is not enough to be modest out of fear, out of the fear that God will punish us if we are immodest or that we will fall into immorality. This is not the obedience of faith. Faith believes that God is good and is eager to obey because it believes that it is good for us, that it is for our happiness. Obedience out of faith will always take us further than obedience out of fear. Fear has its place, especially for the unconverted, but faith in the goodness of God is a more certain ground for morality.

God created men to be aroused by what they see and He created women to be aroused by being seen, these things are good and have a good purpose, they increase the pleasure of the sexual union. As we saw earlier nudity is a type of foreplay. It prepares us to enjoy sex fully; it helps get us in the right frame of mind and body for sex. But what happens when we are constantly seeing and showing almost everything? It starts to lose its effect. There's very little left to see and show in the marriage bed. There is very little left to excite, very little left to arouse, very little left to put us in the right frame of mind and body for great sex.

Some people have had so much 'experience' that a kiss means nothing to them. Through overexposure they have become jaded. Isn't it a sad thing when two people can have their bodies so close that their lips are touching and yet they feel nothing? We realize that something has been lost that was precious. In the same way some men have so glutted their eyes on the female form that a woman's legs or cleavage means nothing to them. Through overexposure they have become so jaded that they feel nothing at the sight of a woman's body. This is not something to shrug off as if it is no big deal. Something precious and irreplaceable has been lost when a man's eyes can go up a woman's legs in the same way they might go up the legs of a cow.

This loss can be seen most pathetically in nudism (or naturism as the preferred term is):

> 'The naked unadorned body, by contrast, is not intrinsically very exciting, especially en masse.... Many visitors to nudist camps report that the sight of all that uncovered flesh brings fatigue and a sense of being slightly unwell. Later, after one gets used to it as the ancients were, it seems nearly banal..... from the earliest times one important function of clothing has been to promote erotic activity...'[5]

Wendy Shalit makes this same point in her book *A Return to Modesty*. She quotes from several men and women who had gone to nudist retreats expecting to be excited but ended up bored and disappointed.[6] Naturists themselves will say that their nudity is not about eroticism[7], it's about body acceptance or liberty or equality or health or the environment. The problem is that nudity is *supposed* to be about eroticism. They are proud of desexualizing nudity but one might as well be proud of taking the color out of a sunset or the sweetness out of a peach.

When a person has seen it all, and become bored with it all, the only thing left is the imagination. This explains why some men make pinups of pictures of women in burqas and why the designer, Hardy Amies, told Prudence Glynn, 'that the most erotic sight of dress he had ever seen was properly garbed nuns playing tennis, wimples and all.'[8] These are women which jaded men can mentally undress in their imaginations and never worry about finding anything disappointing, they can imagine anything they want to imagine including things that *Playboy* could never

5. Lurie, *Language of Clothes*, pp. 212-213.
6. Wendy Shalit, *A Return to Modesty: Discovering the Lost Virtue* (New York: Touchstone, 1999), pp. 173-174.
7. J. C. Flügel in *The Psychology of Clothes* tells us that those who promote nudity claim that nakedness tends to diminish sexuality and that the experience of naturists supports that theory (see p. 109).
8. Glynn, *Skin to Skin*, p. 94.

show them; they can imagine the impossible. It's a sad day when reality has been bled dry of all its pleasures and the only ones left are virtual. Modesty was given to save us from that day.

These experiences regarding nakedness suggest that even if a husband and wife were marooned alone together on a deserted island and there would be no sin in going around naked, they would do best to wear clothes around each other most of the time, so that they could retain the ability to arouse each other by taking off their clothes. In a perfect world this would not be a problem. In a perfect world we could continually enjoy all the sensual pleasures – good food, good sex, good music – without them ever losing their appeal. But, ever since the Fall, sensual pleasures have lost their perfection and now it *is* possible to have too much of a good thing. You may be the biggest lover of ice cream ever, but if you eat ice cream all day every day it won't be long before you are sick of ice cream and never want to see it again. To truly enjoy ice cream takes a measure of self-control because, after a point, the more you eat, the less you enjoy it. What is true of ice cream is also true of other sensual pleasures: self-control and times of self-denial are necessary to keep them pleasurable. This may have been one of the purposes in providing Adam and Eve with clothes. The corruption of their sexuality now meant that they could only be aroused by what they saw and what they showed if there were times when they didn't see it and didn't show it.

Others, from all walks of life, are saying the same thing about this purpose of modesty:

> Rabbi Manis Friedman, 'Modesty is there to preserve intimacy...'[9]

---

9. Manis Friedman, *Doesn't Anyone Blush Anymore? Reclaming Intimacy, Modesty, and Sexuality* (HarperSanFrancisco, 1990), p. 113.

> Sexologist Havelock Ellis: 'The immense importance of feminine modesty in creating masculine passion must be fairly obvious.'[10]
>
> Jewish author Wendy Shalit: '[S]exual modesty may damp down superficial allure, the kind of allure that inspires a one-night stand. But the kind of allure that lasts – this is what modesty protects and inspires.'[11]
>
> Christian author Elizabeth Elliot: 'But I don't want to look at nudity without emotion.... modesty was a system of protection.'[12]
>
> Psychologist J. C. Flügel: 'The real point to bear in mind is that modesty is essentially correlated with desire. Its purpose is to fight desire, but in so doing it rekindles it, so that a circular process is inevitably set in motion.'[13]

Modesty's purpose, then, is not only to keep men from lusting for what they shouldn't have, it is to keep them enthralled with what they do have; modesty is not just a security guard against sexual perversion, it is also a bodyguard for sexual pleasure. Since the Garden of Eden, it has been Satan's chief weapon in temptation to make us believe that what is forbidden is good for the soul, pleasant to the eyes and able to make one happy. We need to tear down his lies with truth, in this case the truth that modesty enhances our experience of sexuality.

---

10. Ellis, *Psychology of Sex*, 1. He is speaking of modesty as reserve, demureness, and it is this quality that makes a woman dress modestly.
11. Shalit, *A Return to Modesty,* p. 172.
12. Elizabeth Elliot, *Let Me Be a Woman: Notes to My Daughter on the Meaning of Womanhood* (Wheaton, IL: Tyndale, 1976), p. 167.
13. J. C. Flügel, *The Psychology of Clothes* (International University Press, 1969), p. 192.

All who love good sex should love modesty, all who want their marriage never to lose its passion should love modesty, all who want one day to enjoy the unparalleled pleasures of the marriage bed should love modesty. And, what is more, we as Christians should sing the praises of the Giver of all good gifts!

10: Masculine Perceptions of Modesty

It should be easy to know how to dress modestly: find out what poses a temptation and don't wear it. Unfortunately, as you already know, it's not that easy. You can ask ten different men and get ten radically different answers. Or, as 'The Rebelution' did, you can ask 1,600 men and get about as many different answers[1]. This may be the most confusing thing about modesty. We can understand why we get different answers about what the end times will be like, for, after all, no one has experienced it personally, but how is it that we can have similar experiences and come to drastically different conclusions based on those experiences? How is it that people agree more on rocket science than on something so basic to everyday life?

Here are some reasons which, though they won't solve the confusion, will at least help explain why it exists:

1. At the time of the printing of this book, this survey appears to have been taken down. The original address was: http://www.therebelution.com/modestysurvey/.

Cause or effect?

One reason is that it is hard to discern between what is an enticement to lust and what is a product of lust. Lust is always caused ultimately by sin in the heart, but when does dress also shoulder some of the blame? When is it that lust is looking for something, anything to latch onto even if it's a woman in a burqa – and lust has managed this feat many times – and when is it that lust is awakened or drawn out by immodesty? When is dress in cahoots with lust and when is lust alone responsible? These are not easy questions to answer.

Differing Motives

Some want to always blame a woman's dress so that they don't have to recognize the full extent of their sin. Others would rather take all the blame than to engage in the unpleasant task of telling the women in their life that they shouldn't wear certain things. Some are afraid of the 'L' word (legalist). Others enjoy criticizing everyone else for immodesty and priding themselves on their superior virtue. Still others enjoy lust and don't want to recognize it for what it is and don't want women to deny them this pleasure. Even worse are those times when a man gets a perverse pleasure from seeing other men checking his wife out and so allows things, which, if he was honest with himself, he knows are immodest. If those who tempt another to sin have a millstone tied around their neck, what will be the lot of those who use the women God has entrusted to their care as bait for the ensnaring of men just to feed their own ego? All of these motives, and many others, colors a man's perspective and influences how he sees modesty.

Differing Sensitivities

Leprosy teaches us that pain can be a blessing. Without pain we can damage our bodies without realizing it. Our consciences function similarly to pain. They tell us when danger is near so we can avoid it before we get hurt. We can, however, in a spiritual case of leprosy, lose our sensitivity to pain. Especially when immersed in a culture where a certain sin is commonplace, it is difficult not to get to the place where it doesn't seem to affect us anymore. Smoking is a good illustration of this principle in the physical realm. Have you ever seen someone take their first puff of a cigarette? They choke and cough like they're about to die (at least they do in the movies, I've never seen it myself). Have you ever seen a chain smoker smoke a cigarette? They find relaxation in the same cigarette. What has changed? Is it that the nicotine has ceased harming their bodies? On the contrary, their lungs show the deadly effects of a lifetime of smoking, but they've gotten used to it and now, instead of cigarettes making them feel bad, they make them feel good. The damage is still being done, but the cigarette doesn't have the immediate effect on them that it used to and so it is easier to be unaware of the danger.

Viewing immodesty can be like this. When we, for the first time, see something we shouldn't see, we may feel an immediate rush that, at the same time it tempts us to keep looking, also clues us in that this is something we shouldn't be looking at, that this is shameful and wrong. But when we've grown up seeing it all our lives, we may be able to look at it and feel nothing. When we can gaze at immodesty unashamedly, then there is nothing to warn us of the damage being done to our souls before it's too late. So the man who rolls his eyes at his brother who is seeking to guard his eyes from things that don't bother him at all may be like the chain smoker who laughs at the boy trying his first cigarette – while priding himself on being 'stronger,' he is only proving that he is 'sicker.' Godly men, with decades-long reputations for purity and godliness, have been accused of having a dirty mind when they seek to address modesty, but it is often precisely because they have a clean mind that they feel the dirtiness of a thing and it could be that it is the dirty minds who can't see anything dirty about it because the dirt feels so natural to them.

It is also possible to be oversensitive to pain, to find ordinary stimuli unbearable. There are neurological problems that cause a person to find the feeling of clothes on their skin immensely painful. Everyday life becomes a nightmare for them because everything bothers them. This also can be true in relation to modesty. It is far less common, but it is possible to become oversensitive to modesty so that anything and everything is seen as a temptation to lust. Though, in general, we should listen to men and what they say, there are exceptions. There are men who, for one reason or another, are not thinking soberly when it comes to modesty. A woman could be dressed in a burqa and some men would still lust after her and claim that she had draped her burqa on in a sexy manner!

Differing Susceptibilities

Men (as well as women) are tempted by different things. What doesn't bother one person at all may be a huge temptation to another person and vice versa. One reason is simply taste. In the same way that some men are more likely to cheat on their diet when offered steak while other men are more likely to cheat when offered ice cream, so some men are likely to cheat on their wife – at least cheat on her in their minds – when confronted with a well-endowed woman in a low-cut dress while other men are more likely to cheat when confronted with a slim woman in tight jeans.

Another reason for the discrepancies is varying levels of testosterone. 'Among men' Gregg Johnson, professor of biology at Bethel College in St. Paul, writes 'there is a strong correlation between testosterone level and sexual activity and aggressive behavior.'[2] Testosterone level varies from man to man and this means that what one man may easily be able to overlook another man may have to exert a lot more energy in fighting. For example, what a seventy-year-old may find a small temptation, a seventeen-year-old may find an intense temptation. Testosterone levels can also vary widely between two men of the same age. Though we must not excuse sin because of our hormones, we can acknowledge that it is a factor in the strength of the battles we face.

Another difference that affects us is background. Someone who was converted later in life and spent decades feeding his flesh may struggle with things that someone converted in childhood who was spared much of the filth that is out there may not struggle with as much.

Marriage is also a large factor. A legitimate outlet for sexual gratification is one of the best defenses against illegitimate gratification. The Bible recognizes this: 'if they cannot exercise self-control, let them marry. For it is better to marry than to burn with passion.' (1 Cor. 7:9). But this outlet is not given to all and it is not given to anyone right away. There is a period of time, often a long period, between the onset of sexual desire and the possibility of marriage and during this window young men are particularly vulnerable to temptation. Then you also have those who are married but are not able, for one reason or another, to enjoy the marriage bed. The vulnerability, for example, of men on business trips is legendary. Perhaps most vulnerable of all are those who are married on paper but divorced in bed because of their spouse's bitter animosity.

All of this means that men (and women) will struggle with lust to varying degrees and their personal struggle with lust

---

2. Johnson, 'Biological Basis for Gender-Specific Behavior' in *Recovering Biblical Manhood and Womanhood*, p. 287.

will influence how they see immodesty. That a man is tempted by a certain way of dressing does not *necessarily* mean that it is immodest, and that a man is not tempted by a certain way of dressing does not *necessarily* mean that it is modest. We should be sensitive to one another's struggles – even if it is not ours – and do what we can to alleviate them. For us to dismiss our brother's struggles and treat him like a legalist or like a monster is unkind and arrogant. Have you ever looked down on someone struggling with something until you were in the same situation and realized for yourself how hard it was? Maybe it was before you had kids and you couldn't understand why a mother with three small children had such a messy house until you had three small children and found yourself wondering how she managed to keep her house so clean! Maybe you had always had good health and couldn't understand why someone with chronic illness was often down until you experienced a lingering illness and then were embarrassed by your lack of compassion. I think many people would be ashamed if they could walk a mile in some other person's shoes and feel how strong the temptation to lust can be and realize how often they have themselves fueled those flames by their dismissive attitude toward immodesty.

Having taken all of this into consideration, it needs to be said that one of the biggest factors in our battle with lust is whether we are killing lust or feeding lust. Are we resisting temptation or are we giving in to temptation? Are we seeking out those things which stir up lust or are we starving lust? We ourselves are often the biggest contributors to our problem and whatever other factors there are, God's grace is more than sufficient for them so that our sin is without excuse.

11: A Survey of Cultural Perceptions of Modesty

Perceptions of modesty vary tremendously from one place to another, from the women of some Muslim communities who are covered from head to toe to the women of some South American tribes who are *exposed* from head to toe. In the next chapter we'll try to make sense of these vastly differing standards, but first let's look a little more closely at the differences themselves.

Examples from Havelock Ellis

Ellis spent the first twenty pages of his multi-volume work *The Psychology of Sex* on 'the various manifestations of modesty.'[1] In those pages he gave close to fifty illustrations of how different cultures perceive modesty drawn from a multitude of original sources as well as his own extensive travels. Here is a sampling:

In the seventeenth century the Naga women of Assam (near India) only concerned themselves with covering their breasts, their logic being that 'it is absurd to cover those parts of the body

1. Ellis, *Psychology of Sex*, p. 8.

which everyone has been able to see from their births, but that it is different with the breasts, which appeared later, and are, therefore, to be covered.'[2]

In Muskat, in the Middle East, it was the face that propriety demanded must especially be kept covered. A man tells about being taken to visit the ladies at the palace where he found that 'their faces were covered with black masks, though the rest of the body might be clothed in a transparent sort of crape; to look at a naked face was very painful for the ladies themselves; even the mother never lifts the mask from the face of her daughter after the age of twelve; that is reserved for her lord and husband.' It was obvious that the sight of his own face was deeply disturbing to them so he donned a mask himself. He writes, 'On making inquiries, I found that my uncovered face was indecent, as a naked person would be to us.'[3]

This is not as uncommon as one might think, there are several similar stories in the Middle East. Ellis tells of an Englishman who came upon a woman bathing in the Euphrates. The woman understandably was very embarrassed, but used her hands to cover her face without taking measures to hide any other part of her body. Ellis adds to this his own experience: 'In Egypt, I have myself seen quite naked young peasant girls, who hastened to see us, after covering their faces.'[4]

And, then, of course, there is the Chinese and the preoccupation they had not long ago with feet: 'Only the husband may see his wife's foot naked. A Chinese woman is as reticent in showing her feet to a man as a European woman

---

2. K. Klemm, 'Peal's Ausflug nach Banpara,' *Zeitschrift fur Ethnologie*, (Heft 5,1898) , p. 334, quoted in Havelock Ellis, *The Psychology of Sex*, p. 14.

3. J.W. Helfer, *Reisen in Vorderasian und Indien, vol. ii*, p. 12, quoted in Havelock Ellis, *The Psychology of Sex*, p. 19.

4. Ellis, *Psychology of Sex*, p. 19.

her breasts.' Ellis opines simply: 'Modesty is a question of convention; Chinese have it for their feet.'[5]

Traveling up the Amazon, it was found that 'among some tribes the women are clothed and the men naked; among others the women naked and the men are clothed.'[6]

Traveling up the Congo, Ellis noticed gradual changes in the dress of women: 'the higher up the river we found ourselves, the higher the dress reached, till it has now, at last, culminated in absolute nudity.'[7]

Ellis observes, interestingly enough, that it seems that the more 'eccentric and arbitrary' the focus of modesty is, the more 'rigid' the devotion to modesty will be. Whereas most people are willing to expose themselves when necessity requires it, in order to be examined by a doctor for example, in many of these places where modesty takes unusual forms it 'possesses the strength of a genuine and irresistible instinct.'[8] One could say that what modesty lacks in sense, it makes up for in zeal.

EXAMPLES FROM ELIZABETH HURLOCK

Hurlock's *The Psychology of Dress* offers several other examples:

> 'In modern Jerusalem, women are considered indecent if any but members of the immediate family should be allowed to view their bare necks. And yet they think nothing of leaving their legs, up to the thighs, exposed when they are sitting down.'[9]

---

5. Ellis, *Psychology of Sex*, p. 20.
6. Ibid., p. 13.
7. Ibid., p. 18.
8. Ibid., p. 71.
9. Elizabeth B. Hurlock, *The Psychology of Dress* (Ronald Press Company, 1929), p. 16.

'With the Carib woman, failure to paint her body is a more serious omission than failure to put on her small leather girdle [author's note: the Caribs are from the Caribbean, in fact that's how the Caribbean got its name]. In the Celebes and Sumatra [Indonesia], exposure of the knee is a sign of indecency, and among some of the tribes of Central Asia, the exposure of the fingertips.'[10]

She summarizes these examples and a few others concluding: 'There is no agreement as to what parts of the body should be covered in deference to modesty. In different nations the head, foot, breast, knees, finger-tips, or genitals are covered, but the part depends upon the people themselves.'[11]

Examples from James Laver

Laver gives some more examples in his books, most notably in *Modesty in Dress*:

'European travelers in the Middle East have often noted that an Arab peasant woman caught in the fields without her veil will throw her skirt over her head, thereby exposing what, to the Western mind, is a much more embarrassing part of her anatomy.'[12]

'In such a sophisticated society as that of eighteenth-century France, while deep décolletage was allowed, it was considered improper to expose the point of the shoulder.'[13]

'In Japan [it is immodest to show] the back of a woman's neck, and in other countries the knees, the navel, the fingertips and other seemingly innocent parts of the female body have been regarded in the same way.'[14]

---

10. Hurlock, *The Psychology of Dress* p. 16.
11. Ibid., p. 16.
12. Laver, *Modesty in Dress*, p. 9.
13. Ibid., p. 9.
14. Ibid., p. 9.

The Greeks thought nothing of men and women exercising together in the nude. In fact, 'gymnasium' originally meant to train while naked.[15] 'The Greeks,' Laver writes, 'unlike their Semitic contemporaries, did not regard nudity as shameful.'[16] The Australian aborigine felt likewise. For him there wasn't a part of the body he was embarrassed to have seen, but he would be 'deeply ashamed if he is seen eating.'[17]

Examples from other writers

According to Wendy Shalit, in Madagascar women can reveal everything but arms.[18] In Zambia, on the other hand, it is legs which should not be revealed. Josh Swiller, a Peace Corp volunteer, tells the story of giving a boy a copy of a *Sports Illustrated* swimsuit issue, something that in the name of 'cultural exchange' he thought was a good idea. He noticed that the boy paid no attention to the cleavage of these women, but was captivated by their thighs. In Zambia, where breast-feeding was done openly but wearing a short skirt could (at some times and in some places) result in stoning, breasts had become a bore while legs and thighs could cause a young man's eyes to 'nearly [fall] out of his head.'[19]

We don't normally think of Eskimos as being immodest, but inside their igloos they evidently are. When they come inside

---

15. gymnasium. Dictionary.com. *Dictionary.com Unabridged*. Random House, Inc. http://dictionary.reference.com/browse/gymnasium (accessed: June 15, 2015).

16. James Laver, *Costume & Fashion: A Concise History* (New York: Thames and Hudson, 1995), p. 30.

17. Laver, *Modesty in Dress*, p. 9.

18. Shalit, *Return to Modesty*, p. 231.

19. Josh Swiller, *Unheard: A Memoir of Deafness in Africa* (New York: Henry Holt and Company, 2007), p. 88.

where it's hot, Pearl Binder writes that men and women go around together completely naked and no one thinks anything about it.[20] In contrast, in Uzbekistan, there is no part of a woman's body that may be seen, not even the mouth or eyes. They wear something called a 'paranchah', which is made from horse hair and looks similar to a black burlap sack, over their heads, allowing them to see out, at least a little, while not allowing others to see in at all. In the past, when women have tried to go out without their paranchah, they have been burned alive.[21]

Even two cultures as closely related as America's and Europe's can have significantly different ideas concerning modesty. One may not feel like America has much sense of modesty left until one travels in Europe where magazine covers are far more lewd and provocative and where women are far more likely to go topless.

I cannot verify that all of these accounts are accurate, in fact, I suspect that many of these writers have made much of little for their own purposes, but no one can deny that concepts of modesty differ from culture to culture, sometimes drastically so. What are we to make of these differences? Havelock Ellis concluded that modesty is an instinct inherent in humans but which morphs into vastly different shapes and forms depending on the societal expectations in the culture in which a person is raised and one form is not any better than another. That is, having something you feel ashamed to expose is fundamental to human nature, but it is as valid to be ashamed of your feet as it is to be ashamed of your genitals, as valid to be reticent about eating publicly as to be reticent about making love publicly. It is nature, so the theory goes, that gives us the capability to feel shame, but

20. Pearl Binder, *Muffs and Morals* (William Morrow & Co.), p. 14.

21. Ibid., p. 14.

it is culture that rightly determines what triggers those feelings of shame. Sociologists and anthropologists have agreed and many Christians have bought into this idea as well.

Are they right? Is modest dress just a cultural issue? This is not an easy question; more ships have sunk on this rock than perhaps any other, but let's see if we can get our bearings in the next chapter.

12: Culture, Modesty and the Christian

Perceptions of modesty do not just change from culture to culture, they also change as a culture changes and this is what most directly concerns us. Our culture's concept of modesty has changed drastically over the last hundred years and it is still changing. In the late 1920s knee length skirts were a scandal, today they are the definition of modesty for many conservative Christians. In 1947 a fashion designer had to hire a stripper to model his bikini because no real model, even in France, would stoop that low. Twenty years later bikinis were mainstream in 'prudish' America and today even Christians can be found wearing them. In the 1980s it was rare to see someone, anyone, marry in a church, any church, in a strapless wedding dress, today it is common in almost all churches. Things are a-changing, but what are we to make of these changes?

In the 1940s C.S. Lewis shared his view in his classic work, *Mere Christianity*, a view which has been influential among Christians today[1]: 'The Christian rule of chastity [author's note: sexual purity] must not be confused with the social rule of "modesty" (in one sense of that word); i.e. propriety, or decency. The social rule of propriety lays down how much of the human body should be displayed … according to the customs of a given social circle. Thus, while the rule of chastity is the same for all Christians at all times, the rule of propriety changes. A girl in the Pacific islands wearing hardly any clothes and a Victorian lady completely covered in clothes might both be equally "modest", proper, or decent, according to the standards of their own societies… I do not think that a very strict or fussy standard of propriety is any proof of chastity or any help to it, and I therefore regard the great relaxation and simplifying of the rule which has taken place in my own lifetime as a good thing.'[2] Lewis believed that sexual purity is governed by Christian rules, as revealed in the Bible, while modesty is governed by social rules, as revealed in the culture where we live. This leads him to agree with the psychologists we quoted in the last chapter that a girl in the Pacific islands may be as modest as a Victorian lady.

Most Christians who follow Lewis in this culture-based definition of modesty will say that there are limits to how far you can go before you have crossed a line. This line is normally drawn someplace where all Christians in our present culture or present circles are in agreement that everything past that is definitely wrong. There may be disagreement about how modest things are on one side of the line, but everyone agrees that anything past that line is definitely immodest. Since everyone agrees on it, it must be true, or at least it is a safe thing to say.

---

1. After this chapter was written, Tim Challies and R. W. Glenn came out with a book, *Modest: Men and Women Clothed in the Gospel,* which teaches a view of modesty largely based on this very quote of Lewis'.

2. C. S. Lewis, *Mere Christianity* (New York: HarperCollins Publishers, 2001), pp. 94-95.

The problem is that this supposed definite line which is not dependent on culture keeps shifting with culture. One hundred years ago Christians might have drawn the line at knee length skirts. Thirty years ago Christians might have drawn the line at strapless gowns. Today the line is often drawn at the bikini[3]. Thirty years from now Christians may be drawing the line at total nudity…or maybe not drawing it at all. So to say that modesty is culturally determined except for everything past a particular line and yet to draw that line in light of our culture is self-defeating.

Furthermore, the very people who draw this line are often the same people who criticize those who draw a more conservative line and call them legalists for drawing such unbiblical lines. If it is unbiblical and legalistic to draw the famous knee length line, how can drawing the bikini line be biblical and gracious? Are we to believe that something can be declared biblical based on

3. In *Modest: Men and Women Clothed in the Gospel,* the authors say that the line (which they call the distinction between modesty and chastity) is a thong bikini: 'Take the thong bathing suit, for example. Apparently, there are some contexts – such as the beaches of Miami, Florida – where these are deemed culturally appropriate. While there, you're unlikely to find anyone looking at you askance for wearing your thong bikini on the beach. But cultural appropriateness is not necessarily the last word. We would argue that, even though in that context the thong bikini does not offend against modesty, it does offend against chastity. This is because the thong bikini has a primary aim that hits the target every time: arousing men.' – Tim Challies and R. W. Glenn, *Modest: Men and Women Clothed in the Gospel* (CruciformPress, 2012), p. 24. (Author's note: Yet, as we have seen, the more commonplace something becomes, the less power it has to affect us and so we can theorize that men who frequent the beaches of Miami get so used to seeing women in thong bikinis that such bathing suits begin to hit their target less and less. So if we take what causes arousal 100% of the time as our line it will prove a remarkably vaporous line.)

overwhelming consensus- especially a consensus which changes every ten years? Obviously not.

To examine the view of modesty as a social construct more closely, let's first remind ourselves of what culture is.

A. Defining Culture

It has been said that the word 'culture' is 'one of the two or three most complex words in the English language....'[4] It can be used in a variety of ways and senses – Webster offers five different definitions for it – it is a word that can be used very broadly or very narrowly.[5] Here we are thinking of it in its broad, comprehensive sense. Terry Eagleton in his book *The Idea of Culture* explains that 'culture can be loosely summarized as the complex of values, customs, beliefs and practices which constitute the way of life of a specific group. It is "that complex whole", as the anthropologist EB Tyler famously puts it in his *Primitive Culture*, "which includes knowledge, belief, art, morals, law, custom, and any other capabilities and habits acquired by man as a member of society".'[6]

That is to say that culture encompasses those traits that are shaped by the world around us rather than those traits with which people are born. Some traits are fundamental to human nature and are found in every culture, but these same traits are often expressed in different ways in different cultures. People in every culture eat, but they don't all like the same foods. Every culture plays, but they don't all find the same recreations enjoyable. They all think something is wrong, but they don't all have the same convictions about what is wrong. Every culture

4. Terry Eagleton, *The Idea of Culture* (Malden, Massachusetts: Blackwell Publishers, 2000), p. 1.

5. Ibid., p. 1.

6. Ibid., p. 34.

has some sense of modesty, but not every culture has the same standards of modesty.

Because culture is the ways and thoughts of a group of people, whatever is true of man will be true of culture. Out of the belief that man is basically good comes the belief that culture is basically good and often the belief that all cultures are equally valid. When we believe that man is fallen and inherently sinful, then we have to understand that culture, every culture, is fallen and inherently sinful. Recognizing culture's bent to evil, we must be on the alert to its influence on our lives, even those aspects which seem to be part of the very fabric of our being. If our culture gives us a preference for apple pie over roasted grasshoppers, no problem, but when it gives us a seemingly innate sense of what is right and wrong we have to defer to the Bible's greater wisdom, even if it makes us appear un-American or un-Asian or un-African. In the past the world – and too often the church – was guilty of thinking that its own cultural values were necessarily and automatically superior to those of other cultures. Today our world – and too often the church – has gone to the opposite extreme: we are afraid to call anything wrong that is a part of someone's culture.

D. A. Carson does a masterful job of explaining the good and the bad we find in culture: '…it comes as an enormous relief to recognize that, however odious and sweeping sin is, whether in personal idolatry or in its outworking in the barbarities of a Pol Pot or an Auschwitz, God intervenes to restrain evil, to display his 'common grace' to and through all, so that glimpses of glory and goodness disclose themselves even in the midst of the wretchedness of rebellion. God still sends his sun and rain upon the just and the unjust; he still guides the surgeon's hand and gives strength to the person who picks up the garbage; the sunset still takes our breath away, while a baby's smile steals our hearts. Acts of kindness and self-sacrifice surface among every race and class of human beings, not because we are simple mixtures of good and evil, but because even in the midst of our deep rebellion God restrains us and displays his glory and his goodness.... Christians cannot long think about Christ and culture without reflecting on the fact that this is *God's* world, but that this side of the fall this world is simultaneously resplendent with glory and awash in shame, and that every expression of human culture simultaneously discloses that we were made in God's image and shows itself to be mis-shaped and corroded by human rebellion against God'[7]

To rephrase D. A. Carson, we could say that our society's perception of modesty shows both that man is made in God's image and that man has been mis-shaped and corroded by human rebellion against God. To accept our culture's view of modesty indiscriminately, then, will be to accept, not only those things which are 'resplendent with glory' but also those things which are 'awash in shame.'

B. Culture and Application of Biblical Principles

I suspect that one reason behind the view that sexual purity is nonnegotiable while modesty shifts with the shifting sands of social mores is most likely that the Bible spells out several sexual sins (premarital sex, homosexuality, adultery) but doesn't spell out the sins of modesty. We already spent a chapter on how God's Word gives principles that guide and govern us even where God's Word does not give specifics. Let's now look at some other biblical principles, noting how these principles are fleshed out by various cultures and then ask ourselves if it really is safe and reasonable to believe that culture plays such a defining role in applying biblical principles.

---

7. D. A. Carson, *Christ and Culture Revisited* (Grand Rapids, Michigan: Wm. B. Eerdmans Publishing Co, 2008), p. 49.

Diligence

The Bible teaches that diligence is good and laziness is bad, but it doesn't spell out exactly what it means to be diligent. Should we infer, then, that the difference between the two is culturally determined? Should we look to our culture's standard of diligence and measure ourselves by it in order to discern whether we are obeying the Bible's commands to be diligent? If so, in some places it would be very easy to be diligent! Do we have no right to exhort someone to work hard if, according to their peers, they are putting in the effort expected of them? After all, if the Pacific girl is just as modest as the Victorian lady, then the teenager who spends as much time on the job texting as he does working may be just as diligent as the one who puts his whole mind and body into the job. They both may be living up to their societal norms and the Bible doesn't tell them exactly how hard they have to work in order to be diligent. American culture is becoming less and less hard-working. Are we as Christians allowed to become less and less hard-working as well as long as we are as hard-working as the people around us? We're allowing ourselves to become less and less modest after all, why not less diligent?

Sexual Purity

Besides forbidding sex outside of marriage, the Bible doesn't say much on what is permissible between two unmarried members of the opposite sex. *How far is too far* is one of the hot questions of the day, even hotter than the *how short is too short* question. Should we look to our culture to figure this out? Is anything short of intercourse okay for two unmarried people as long as society accepts it? Is it okay, as we asked earlier, for a woman to flirt with another man's husband?

I have purposely chosen areas where Christians in our culture still understand something of what biblical principles require of us. We know instinctively that these things are wrong even though some cultures say they are fine and the Bible doesn't directly contradict them. But can we always expect that to be the case? Will Christians always understand what is right and wrong even when their culture is filling their minds with lies? Let's look at some examples of what Christians in other cultures have believed about right and wrong.

Slavery

For quite some time many Christians saw nothing wrong with slavery. The Bible not only doesn't forbid slavery, it actually permits it, although there are many principles in the Word of God that should have made it obvious that slavery as it was practiced in the 18th and 19th centuries was immoral and unjust. Kidnapping innocent people and shipping them halfway around the world in deadly conditions to be treated in many cases as little more than cattle just because of the color of their skin has to be one of the most appalling atrocities that has ever been condoned among Christian people. And yet for many years it was condoned by almost everyone. Not only did Christians accept slavery in theory, they often owned slaves and, occasionally, even were slave traders themselves, as was temporarily the case with John Newton. It wasn't that it was so hard to figure out that this form of slavery was wrong; it was that the cost of acting on that knowledge was so high. It would upset their whole way of life to abolish slavery, they couldn't even imagine functioning without it, so they turned a blind eye to its injustices and came up with elaborate justifications. It wasn't the Bible that was dark and hard to understand, it was man's mind – yes, even the Christian mind – that was dark and loathe to understand.

Intellectual Property

We all know that stealing is wrong, the Bible is clear on that, but is plagiarism wrong? Is producing and buying pirated copies of material wrong? To most of us I imagine these actions are obviously stealing, but not all Christians see it that way. I spent a few weeks in Africa and while there I graded some papers written by seminary students. Many of the papers included material that had been copied wholesale from theological books and presented as their own. In some cases half the paper would be a plagiarism of a theological book. Few of them seemed to think anything about it. This is how they had always been writing papers. Their culture doesn't frown on plagiarism in the same way as ours does, does that mean it was okay for them?

I also spent time in an Asian country where Christians thought nothing of buying pirated movies and software. I talked with an American who'd been there over twenty years and he told me he had been trying to convince them it was wrong and yet he knew of very few Christians in the country who had any qualms about it. Most of them claimed that it was part of being a good steward of God's money. To them it seemed ludicrously extravagant to pay $20 for the official software or movie when they could get the pirated edition for two dollars. Most of these people weren't desperately poor; they were just used to picking up new software the way we might pick up a new magazine whenever it caught our eye.

Worse, still, some Christians in that country produced and sold pirated copies of Christian books, making money at the expense of other Christians. It was hard to make even *seminary students* buy the non-pirated versions of the theological books required for their classes! I even knew missionaries who had started to buy the pirated materials. These Christians weren't doing anything wrong in the eyes of people around them and the

Bible doesn't lay out a doctrine of intellectual property, so does that mean it was okay for them? They didn't feel instinctively that these things were wrong in the way we do and even when confronted with biblical principles they weren't convinced, not because the truth was unconvincing, but because it was too costly to be convinced.

This is usually why it is hard to know what is right and wrong: we don't want to know. We like things the way they are and don't want to know if we should change. It would be too hard, too costly, too inconvenient. We are good at coming up with justifications for what we want to do, even spiritually sounding and biblically flavored justifications. At such times Satan can appear as an angel of light. He used Scripture to try to get Jesus to sin and he can use Scripture to try to get us to sin. We need to follow Jesus' example and respond to such arguments with 'it is written again.' To those who say that slavery of blacks is Scripturally sanctioned, we say, 'it is written again, Do unto others as you would have them do unto you.' To those who say that buying pirated media is part of being a good steward, we say, 'it is written again, Woe to him who builds his house by unrighteousness and his chambers by injustice, who uses his neighbor's service without wages and gives him nothing for his work....' (Jer. 22:13).

And, when others argue that dressing according to the growing immodesty of our age is acceptable in order to 'be in the world' or in order to 'not go beyond what Scripture teaches,' we can say, 'it is written again, do not be conformed to this world, but be transformed by the renewal of your mind, that you may discern what is that good, acceptable and perfect will of God.' John Wesley, speaking of Romans 12:2 in a sermon on dress, says: 'Indeed this exhortation relates more directly to the *wisdom* of the world, which is totally opposite to his "good and acceptable and perfect will." But it likewise has a reference even to the *manners* and *customs* of the world, which naturally flow from its wisdom and spirit and are exactly suitable thereto.'[8]

I hope these things help overcome what is often regarded as the unanswerable objection to modesty. If someone expresses concern over some form of immodesty, there seems to always be someone who will pipe up with, 'Well, you know, some people would say you are immodest because you're showing x (your wrists, your ankles, etc).' as if this argument was a tower of unassailable truth. But this tower is built on sinking sand. It assumes that all standards are equally valid. The person who believes a woman can't even show her eyes is just as legitimate as the person who believes a woman shouldn't go topless. It would be like someone expressing grief over a heinous case of child abuse and someone else shrugging it off by saying, 'Well, you know, in some places people would say you are abusive because you smack your child's hand when he tries to touch a hot stove.' Once we stop to think about it like this, we realize that such an argument is sadly lacking in logic. It is sobering how easily we can be suckered in by a groundless argument when it provides a rationale for what we already want to believe.

God's Word does not give specific answers to every question we have, but as we resist the influence of our culture around us and saturate our minds and hearts in God's Word, the answers will become clearer.

C. Societal Rules of Modesty Are Pharisaical and Self-Contradictory

Many people seem to think that if we say that our standards of modesty should not be governed by culture then we will all end up wearing a burqa. This assumes that if modesty doesn't change

8. John Wesley, 'On Dress,' in *The Works of John Wesley* (Grand Rapids, MI: Baker, 1979 [1872]) quoted in David Vaughan and Diane Vaughan, *The Beauty of Modesty*, p. 212.

from culture to culture then we have to follow the example of the society with the highest standards; since there is only one right answer, we figure all the wrong answers will be those which fall short of the right answer. If sin is missing the mark, surely it misses because it aims too low. However, in fact, as often as not, in rebelling against God's law, people require more than God requires. The Pharisees were the quintessential example of this.

The Pharisees were continually criticizing Jesus and His disciples for 'transgressing the tradition of the elders'; they didn't wash their hands before eating (Matt. 15:2), they plucked grain on the Sabbath (Matt. 12:1-2), they ate with sinners (Matt. 9:11). On the surface of things the Pharisees didn't require less than God required, they required more. Jesus revealed them as the hypocrites they were by showing that in obeying the rules of the elders they were guilty of breaking the laws of God. They said you could devote money to God which absolved you of any responsibility to care for your aging parents (Mark 7:9-13). They had many rules about washing hands and dishes and meanwhile their own hearts were full of filth (Mark 7:1-23). They were willing to pull an ox out of the ditch on the Sabbath, but unwilling for a man to be healed on the same day (Matt. 12:10-12). They strained gnats while swallowing camels; they rejected the commandment of God in favor of keeping the tradition of men (Mark 7:8-9). Rebellion against God's law does not necessarily result in the absence of law; more often it takes the form of creating our own laws, thereby making ourselves God. This is the portrait of the Pharisees.

It is also a portrait of many of those cultures with very high standards of modesty. In light of this, it isn't so surprising that there are women who use their skirts to cover their faces while neglecting to worry about the rest of their bodies. They have replaced God's laws with the traditions of men. Even those 'modest' Victorians C.S. Lewis talked about were guilty as Prudence Glynn writes, '[A]t the high point of hypocrisy in dress, the mid-Victorian age, very respectable women went about in, and indeed were commanded to appear in Court in, décolletages which we would consider extremely risqué, while the mention of legs was unpardonable and the sight of an ankle deeply moving.'[9]

By saying that modesty is not based on social norms, we not only provide a framework to say that what is socially acceptable is immodest, we also have a basis to say that what is socially required is over-modest. Now, I think we can all agree that it is not sinful to dress over-modestly, if the standard is knee length, no one is going to rebuke you for wearing something ankle length. We shouldn't require it of others, but it is not sinful to do it ourselves and at times it may be a part of being all things to all people.

Not only do cultures break God's law in keeping their rules, but often their own rules are self-contradictory. They can't even be consistent in their own rebellion. Most cultures have different standards of modesty for different groups of people. For instance, as Alison Lurie points out, married and single women: 'In the 1900s...evening fashions for unmarried girls were sharply distinguished from fashions for matrons and spinsters.... The unmarried girl who appeared in an evening dress such as her mother might wear with perfect propriety – a low-cut, jet-trimmed, ruby-red or emerald-green satin, for instance – was considered either very fast or very badly brought up. Today the signals have been reversed. Well-bred girls go dancing in revealing costumes of neon red, orange and green. Their mothers, on the other hand, wear modestly cut party clothes in the same limited

9. Glynn, *Skin to Skin*, p. 52.

range of colors they favor for day: brown, tan, black, white and pale or navy blue. One possible reason for this change is that there has been a shift in sexual morality. Aristocratic Edwardians, though they paid lip service to virtue and demanded virginity before marriage, condoned a discrete promiscuity afterwards. Today well-born young women, like the female young of some Polynesian tribes, are tacitly allowed to sleep around and even live around a bit before marriage. After the wedding, however, they are expected to behave themselves or get out.'[10]

Cultures also often have different standards for different socioeconomic levels, sometimes allowing the wealthy to get away with things the lower classes can't. A mistress in Victorian England could, with perfect social propriety, wear provocative dresses which would have gotten her servant girl labeled all sorts of names. A nobleman in Tudor England could wear indecently short jackets which would have earned a yeoman a fine of twenty shillings. At other times, the lower classes can get away with what the wealthy can't, as Shiu-Sian Angel Hsu writes concerning some interpretations of Islamic dress: 'In several schools of law there is the opinion that for slavegirls the breast is not considered awra [author's note: those parts of the body which are intimate and must be kept out of sight], whereas for free women, it is.'[11]

As well, cultures usually have different standards of modesty for different settings. In the Victorian era what would be scandalous in the daytime, indeed what could get you arrested for indecent exposure when the sun was up, could be worn to an evening ball and receive approval and admiration. In our own

---

10. Lurie, *Language of Clothes*, p. 253.

11. Shiu-Sian Angel Hsu, *Dress in Islam: Looking and Touching in Hanafi Fiqh* (Ph.D. Diss., University of Utah, 1994) quoted in Yedida Kalfon Stillman, *Arab Dress: From the Dawn of Islam to Modern Times: A Short History* (Leiden, Netherlands: Brill, 2000), p. 37.

day, people can wear things to proms that would be frowned upon, if not forbidden, at school or work. And certainly, parts of the body that are exposed by almost everyone at the beach are not acceptable to expose most other places.

Another thing to keep in mind is that a sense of modesty is not always behind what is considered to be appropriate and inappropriate in dress. A woman may be embarrassed to be caught in a robe and curlers, but it is not an embarrassment out of modesty. A woman who wouldn't be embarrassed to go around in a miniskirt but wants to crawl under a rock when she finds her slip is hanging half an inch below a boot length skirt is not embarrassed because she is immodest, but because she has committed a social faux pas. These differences are easier to discern in our own culture, but when it comes to cultures we're not familiar with, we often mistake other social issues for modesty. Islamic dress is known for being one of the most 'modest' yet even it is often not about modesty. Islamic dress is far from a homogeneous mixture, but here are some views on what motivates it at least in some places at sometimes:

Fadwa El Guindi, professor at the University of Southern California, writes:

> '...veiling in contemporary Arab culture is largely about identity, largely about privacy-of space and body. I contend that the two qualities, modesty and seclusion, are not adequate characterizations of the phenomenon as it is expressed in the Middle East.'[12]

Yedida Kalfon Stillman, who was professor of History and Near Eastern Languages at the University of Oklahoma until her death and has been called 'the world's acknowledged expert on Islamic

12. Fadwa El Guindi, *Veil: Modesty, Privacy and Resistance* (Berg, 1999), xvii.

clothing' believed that while Islamic distinctive dress served several purposes, one of the most basic was to distinguish the Muslim from the non-Muslim at a glance.[13]

One of those other purposes was to signal status. Stillman speaks of the nineteenth century move towards modernization and unveiling and why so many women resisted this change: '...veiling had always been an indicator of social class, and traditionally not only peasant villagers, but "many of the women of the lower orders"... went about in public unveiled.'[14]

And, of all things, even fashion is said to be behind the wearing of the veil! Stillman quotes a study that showed that 40 percent of educated women surveyed in Egypt said that they wore Islamic dress 'because it was the latest fashion.'[15]

Nesta Ramazani writes in the *Journal of South Asian and Middle Eastern Studies* that '... all of the present-day manifestations of veiling share one common thread; namely, "the need to reassert cultural identity."'[16.]

It seems difficult, let alone dangerous, to consider modesty a cultural issue when cultural views are so obviously self-contradicting and hypocritical – and sometimes not about modesty at all! They pretend to build the wall of modesty with one hand and with the other hand they are tearing down the very wall they are building. Is this really the compass we want to set our course by? You might as well say there is no such thing as modesty at all as to say that at one time of day modesty is this and at another time it is that, for one person in a society it means this and for another person in the same society it means that.

13. Yedida Kalfon Stillman, *Arab Dress: From the Dawn of Islam to Modern Times: A Short History* (Leiden, Netherlands: Brill, 2000), p. 1.

14. Ibid., p. 154.

15. Ibid., p. 159.

16. Nesta Ramazani, 'The Veil- Piety or Protest?' *Journal of South Asian and Middle Eastern Studies 7:2* (1983), 36, quoted in Stillman, *Arab Dress*, p. 158.

Standards of modesty are not only inconsistent across cultures, they are even inconsistent within cultures.

These things are not to say that culture should play no part in our clothing choices. Once we have exercised sober judgment to discern the best we can which clothes are modest, which clothes cover all our 'unpresentable parts', we can and should then consult our culture to choose which of these modest clothes would be most culturally appropriate for a particular place or a particular situation. As society changes over the years we may choose differently within these confines of modesty, yet our convictions of which parts of the body are acceptable and unacceptable for public view, must not be allowed to change in tandem with culture.

D. Modesty Is Not Governed By Societal Norms

As we saw in an earlier chapter, modesty cannot be understood apart from sexuality. If we were not sexual beings, modesty would make no sense. *The Westminster Catechism* acknowledges this fact when it categorizes immodesty as a breaking of the command not to commit adultery. John Calvin, in his commentary on I Timothy, also acknowledges this when he speaks of immodesty as a 'want of chastity' and as a 'departure from chastity.'[17] This reality is also reflected in the correlation between a society's sexual mores and its modesty, for, in general,

17. John Calvin has in mind immodesty in the sense of excess and extravagance, which is what I Timothy 2:8-10, the passage he is commenting on, expressly forbids. But if it is a departure from chastity to wear clothes which are opulent and draw attention to one's wealth, how much more is it a departure from chastity to wear clothes which are revealing and draw attention to one's body? It is also true that Calvin writes: '...since dress is an indifferent matter, (as all outward matters are,) it is difficult to assign a fixed limit, how far we ought to go.' In understanding his meaning, it is helpful to again remember that he is speaking in the context of the quality/expense of clothes. Whether our clothes are cotton or silk is generally a matter indifferent.

increasing immorality is accompanied by increasing immodesty. As goes sexuality, so goes modesty, such is the close relationship between the two.

There is, undeniably, much room for hypocrisy and many societies which practice modesty and proclaim morality do not live up to the way they dress and talk. But, after all, why do police imposters wear uniforms? Is it not because real policemen wear uniforms? Is not this also why counterfeit money looks so much like real money? Hypocrites are sure to try to hide their hypocrisy by following as closely as possible the appearance of the real thing. The fact that cultures sometimes try to hide their immorality behind a veneer of modesty only shows that real sexual purity is modest.

C.S. Lewis was wrong to divorce modesty from sexual purity. Sexual purity is so crucial to modesty – and modesty to sexual purity – that to separate the two is to disembowel modesty and leave it to wither away. If we don't look to culture for our standards in sexual purity, even in those areas not specifically mentioned in Scripture, such as flirting with another woman's husband and pornography, why should we take its standards of modesty and immodesty? Modesty, then, is not governed by societal norms because it is an aspect of sexuality, which is not governed by societal norms. It is rooted in realities such as man's need for Christ's righteousness, the beauty of the human body and the God-given male-female distinctions, realities which transcend cultures, transcend countries and transcend centuries, and so it is that modesty transcends cultures, countries, centuries.

The fact that cultures have different perceptions of modesty is only an indication that cultures are not perfectly guided by God's ways and words. It would be more surprising if different cultures *didn't* have different views of modesty. Because sexual immorality and immodesty often go hand-in-hand, we should be especially wary of taking the standards of a culture that is becoming increasingly immoral, such as our own culture.

After writing that 'the use and manner of clothes is a mark of the state of a man's mind' the eighteenth century pastor William Law went on to say, 'To pretend to make the way of the world our measure in these things, is as weak and absurd, as to make the way of the world the measure of our sobriety, abstinence, or humility. It is a pretense that is exceedingly absurd in the mouths of Christians, who are to be so far from conforming to the fashions of this life, that to have overcome the world, is made an essential mark of Christianity.'[18]

If we stop to think about it, there is evidence that we know instinctively that the way of the world should not be our measure of modesty. When we visit a foreign country we feel free to eat with chopsticks (or at least try to!), free to bow instead of shaking hands, free to try our hand at cricket. It may not always be easy, it may feel strange or uncomfortable, but we are willing, or at least should be willing, to do our best. However, when we travel to a place where women go topless on the beaches or where the natives go around in nothing more than a loincloth, we don't feel free to do the same; it's not just that it feels strange or uncomfortable, it feels wrong. It takes years, and sometimes generations, of our culture embracing a form of immodesty before we gradually become accustomed to it. Even if you haven't thought of it, you know that modesty is not a neutral aspect of culture; it is part of God's law written on your heart.

Pastor Robert Spinney writes:

> 'Despite this [universal realization that nakedness is humiliating], our sinful minds dilute and our sinful wills suppress these

---

18. William Law, *A Serious Call to a Devout and Holy Life* quoted in David Vaughan and Diane Vaughan, *The Beauty of Modesty*, p. 214.

> God-given moral sensibilities. It used to be that people living in the Judeo-Christian West wore ample clothing while the unreached tribal peoples featured in National Geographic magazines were almost naked. As Christian cultural influence wanes in the West, however, we are looking more and more like the unreached tribal peoples.'[19]

If these truths are written on our hearts, why do so few Christians take them seriously? Could it be for the same reason that Christians haven't always taken what God says about stealing and slavery seriously? Because it would cost us more than we want to pay? We may not know exactly where implementing these principles will take us but I think we know the general direction and we suspect it will take us farther down that road than would be comfortable. It may cost us our favorite clothes. It may earn us reproach and ridicule, even from other Christians. The problem with modesty is not that it's so unclear, though there is an element of that, the real problem is that it has the potential of being so uncomfortable.

There is no easy way to figure out exactly where the line is between what is modest and what is immodest (anymore than between what is diligent and what is lazy), but let us not in a desire for easy answers be duped by answers which are self-defeating – socially-defined answers which, by disorientating our compasses, allow us to be comfortable with where we are at now but in the end sweep us up in the tide of our society's degeneration.

---

19. Spinney, *Dressed to Kill,* p. 25.

13: Obedience Brings Light

Jesus said, '…to everyone who has, more will be given, and he will have abundance; but from him who does not have, even what he has will be taken away.' (Matt. 25:29). The idea is that if we take care of what is entrusted to us, we will be entrusted with more, but if we squander what God has entrusted us with, He will take away what we had to begin with. This is a principle that is true of many things, including knowledge: *if we obey what we know, we will know more, but if we disobey what we know, we will know less.* Samuel Rutherford puts it this way, 'If we had more practice of obedience, we should have more sound light.'[1]

Let's look at an example as it relates to modesty. Your conscience tells you that a skirt should be at least 'x' long to be modest. But then you see the cutest skirt ever and it looks great on you and it's on sale, plus you've been shopping all day and you haven't found anything, you'll just go ahead and buy

1. Samuel Rutherford, *Letters of Samuel Rutherford* (Edinburgh: Banner of Truth Trust, 1973), p. 129

it. It's not shockingly immodest, it's just not quite up to your normal standards. So you wear it, ignoring or rationalizing away any reservations your conscience is whispering in your ear. After wearing it a while, it no longer seems edgy at all, it looks completely modest to you. You buy others of that length. Time goes by and you see another skirt that you fall in love with which is a little shorter still. A couple of years ago you would have never dreamed of wearing such a short skirt, but now it doesn't look so bad. You'll just be very careful when you sit, it will be fine, you tell yourself. And so a little more light is squandered away leaving darkness in its place, darkness that encroaches inch by inch on your standards of modesty. What you had has been taken away from you.

But it is also true that 'to everyone who has, more will be given.' As you are faithful to your 'x' long standard of modesty even when it seems impossible to find any that length, even when 'everyone else' is wearing them shorter, more light will be given you. You may start to weed out a few things that you used to wear without a second thought. Or you may start to see that things you had always been taught were immodest are modest after all. Increased light does not necessarily cause a person to raise their standards. There have been occasions when I have lowered my standards as I grew in my understanding of modesty, though usually the changes have been in the other direction.

This principle of obedience is one of the most important keys to understanding modesty. Without a consistent living by your convictions, everything else this book has said will not likely bear good fruit in your life. This is not only true for women making their own clothing choices, it is also true for fathers and husbands who are tempted by the complaints of their daughters and wives to compromise their convictions by what they allow to be worn by members of their household. If you get nothing else from this book, I hope you will be determined to never compromise your standards of modesty, however tempting the situation, however costly the obedience, however much flak you take for it. Don't think that you can ignore the light for a moment and then go back to living the way you were. Every time you go against your conscience, you harden your conscience. If you compromise a little, you will soon compromise a lot – and never realize it.

Josh Harris writes in regard to lust, but it is equally relevant to immodesty, 'Don't grow weary. Consistency in the little areas will slowly strengthen you spiritually. Just as compromise adds up, so your faithful investments into holiness will grow too.'[2] Every time you resist the temptation to wear something that is a little shorter, a little lower, a little tighter, a little more attention-grabbing than you think you should, it is an 'investment in holiness' and in understanding as well.

It is also dangerous to think of our faithfulness to modesty as hermetically sealed off from the rest of our spiritual and moral life. We don't live compartmentalized lives, with our prayer life in one compartment, our relationships with others in another compartment, with our personal integrity in a compartment over here and our modesty in a compartment over there. Whatever we do in one area affects all other areas of our life. What is true of the guilt of sin ('For whoever shall keep the whole law, and yet stumble in one point, he is guilty of all'- James 2:10) is true of the effect of sin as well.

This means that, on the one hand, anything that keeps our hearts from being right will keep us from thinking rightly about modesty, even if it is something as seemingly disconnected as bitterness or dishonesty or coldness to God. On the other hand, this also means that when we compromise our convictions

2. Harris, *Sex Is Not the Problem (Lust Is)*, p. 78.

regarding modesty, we don't just darken our minds in regards to modesty, all of our spiritual life is affected. Our relish for spiritual things, our prayer life, our heart for the lost, all will be affected.

Jonathan Edwards, in his classic *Religious Affections*, speaks of how having the right heart disposition will often help us discern between what is good and bad better than being intellectually bright but lacking such a heart. A pure heart is naturally inclined to what is pure. It will often know instinctively when something is impure even if it cannot put its finger on what makes it impure. This is not to say we should always trust our heart, for our hearts are never completely pure, but it does mean that if we want to know the difference between what is right and wrong, pure and impure, modest and immodest, we must pay as much attention to getting our hearts right as we do to getting our thinking right.

Here is a summary sentence from Edwards, the whole quote being included in the footnotes[3], 'So an eminently humble, or

---

3. 'A holy disposition and spiritual taste, where grace is strong and lively, will enable the soul to determine what actions are right and becoming Christians, not only more speedily but far more exactly than the greatest abilities without it... He has, as it were, a spirit within him that guides him. The habit of his mind is attended with a taste by which he immediately relishes that air and mien which is benevolent, and disrelishes the contrary. It causes him to distinguish between one and the other in a moment, more precisely than the most accurate reasonings can find out in many hours. The nature and inward tendency of a stone or other heavy body that is let fall from aloft, shows the way to the centre of the earth more exactly in an instant than the ablest mathematician, without it, could determine by his most accurate observations, in a whole day. Thus it is that a spiritual disposition and taste teaches and guides a man in his behavior in the world. So an eminently humble, or meek, or charitable disposition, will direct a person of mean capacity to such a behaviour, as is agreeable to Christian rules of humility, meekness and charity, far more readily and precisely than the most diligent study

meek, or charitable disposition, will direct a person of mean capacity [i.e. someone who is not very smart] to such a behaviour, as is agreeable to Christian rules of humility, meekness and charity, far more readily and precisely than the most diligent study and elaborate reasonings of a man of the strongest faculties, who has not a Christian spirit within him.'

Edwards was certainly not belittling the careful study of God's Word; he was, after all, one of the greatest theologians of his time. It would be folly to think that as long as we focus on our hearts, we don't need to be diligent students of God's Word, for God Himself must have thought differently since He gave us His Word! And, among other things, the Word of God is a mirror showing us what is in our hearts. Yet this does help to explain why things do not always seem crystal clear in the Bible. It is not the Bible that is imperfect or dark, it is our hearts.

I suppose anyone who desires to live by God's Word has been frustrated at one time or another that it doesn't address some issue

---

and elaborate reasonings of a man of the strongest faculties, who has not a Christian spirit within him.... The saints, in thus judging of actions by a spiritual taste, have not a particular recourse to the express rules of God's word, with respect to every word and action that is before them, the good or evil of which they thus judge: but yet their taste itself, in general, is subject to the rule of God's word, and must be tried by that, and a right reasoning upon it. As a man of a healthy palate judges of particular morsels by his taste; but yet his palate itself must be judged of, whether it be healthier or no, by certain rules and reasons. But a spiritual taste of soul mightily helps the soul in its reasonings on the Word of God, and in judging of the true meaning of its rules: for it removes the prejudices of a depraved appetite, and naturally leads the thoughts in the right channel. It casts a light on the Word of God, and causes the true meaning most naturally to come to mind, through the harmony there is between the disposition and relish of a sanctified soul and the true meaning of the rules of God's Word.' – Jonathan Edwards, *The Religious Affections* (Edinburgh: Banner of Truth Trust, 2001), pp. 209-210.

about which they need direction. Maybe you have felt that way in regards to modesty. You would wear whatever God wanted if He would just tell you. Why doesn't He speak more plainly? There are paragraphs and paragraphs devoted to how to tell if such and such a mold is a spreading mold or not and what to do in either case. Why not at least a sentence giving some details on modesty? Why, for that matter, when we ask God for wisdom in some area, whether it is modesty or parenting or theology, doesn't He quickly open our eyes and give us all the answers? Why does growing in wisdom usually result in seeing more sin in our own hearts and feeling less and less like we have it all together?

God's normal way of giving wisdom is little by little and is linked with His purifying work in our hearts. As we grow in faith, humility, love, we also grow in knowledge, understanding, wisdom. We often think we just need to know what we should do and don't realize how much we still need to grow into what we should be. God has joined these two things together and has not made them an instantaneous event, but a lifetime journey.

Let's take a person, maybe a hypocrite, who is proud and self-righteous. If the Bible told that person the humble thing to do or say in every situation, he would probably do it, at least most of the time, just so he would be thought humble, but it wouldn't make him truly humble. Yet when he becomes truly humble, he won't have to be given detailed instruction on how to act humble in every situation he encounters, he will act humbly because he is humble! This may be why God doesn't spell many things out – He doesn't want us to know perfectly how to go through the motions of living righteously apart from a heart for righteousness. Now there are things God has spelled out, and we should obey those things even when we don't feel like it, even when our hearts aren't in it. A bad heart is a reason to repent, not an excuse to disobey.

I don't suppose anyone has ever figured out exactly what it looks like to dress modestly, but that does not mean we cannot grow in our understanding of it. This book has sought to be a lodestone to your conscience by bringing God's Word to bear on the question of modesty. In so far as it has done so accurately, you are responsible for what you have learned. How you respond will have serious and far-reaching ramifications in all aspects of your Christian walk. Disobedience is dangerous because of Who it is we are disobeying. Modesty is not society's idea, not the church's idea, not my idea – modesty is God's idea.

If you are confused about what you should do and how you should dress, if you are worried that you may inadvertently be doing the wrong thing, take comfort. As you seek God and seek to live in the light He has given you, He will keep you and guide you and give you more light. Maybe you see how far short you fall in seeking Him as you should, yet, though your seeking be imperfect, the God you seek is perfectly perfect and will keep His promise to guide His children in the paths of righteousness for His name's sake. We're not going to make it safely to the end because we made all the right decisions along the way; we're going to make it because Jesus Christ is interceding for us and because God the Father is working in us to will and to do of His good pleasure and because the Holy Spirit has sealed us, guarantying our inheritance with the saints in heaven. Though many things may be dark and mysterious till the day we die, this hope is clear and sure.

14: Brussels Sprouts, Brownies and Modesty

This book was originally part of a much larger project and addressed such questions as: What is fashion and how did it come to be what it is now? Why is skimpy clothing so often more potent and dangerous than outright nudity? How should we interact with other Christians who have dramatically different standards of modesty than we do? These are worthwhile questions and hopefully that material will find its way into another book someday, but one of the main goals of this book has been to show how beautiful and desirable and conducive to happiness modesty is. How you think of modesty in general plays such a large role in how you work it out in its specifics and, in particular, whether you are always trying to get away with less or whether you want to have as much as you can.

It boils down to whether you think of modesty as brownies or Brussels sprouts. Is it something you delight in or something you only do because you know you have to? When someone tells you there is more to be had, do you rejoice or do you whine? When you love modesty as much as most people love brownies, you are well on your way to dressing modestly.

It has been in the interest of creating a brownie-like view of modesty that we have seen how:

-Modesty is a reminder of the provision of Christ's righteousness to meet our desperate need.

- Fundamental to true Christian modesty is the belief that our bodies are incredibly good, incredibly beautiful.

-A woman's body in particular is a garden of delights and modesty is the fence, charming as white pickets and daunting as barbed wire, protecting it from being treated as a public amusement park and preserving it as a private garden for her husband alone.

-Modesty is a bodyguard for sexual pleasure even more than it is a security guard against sexual perversion, keeping us enthralled with what we do have instead of lusting for what we don't have.

Having been given such a good gift by such a good Father, let us treat it like a good gift and not like a gift no one wants. Instead of crying that we have to eat three whole ones and making any number of excuses why that is unreasonable, let us be happy that we are shown such generosity and lick the plate clean. Let's be those who treat modesty like brownies and ask if we have had all that we can... for, unless I miss my guess by a long shot, there is a lot more out there to be had!

Selected Bibliography

Christian Literature on Modesty (Contemporary)

Banda, Raphael and Namukolo. *Your Dressing Matters!* Lusaka, Zambia: Evergreen Publishers, 2008.

Challies, Tim and RW. Glenn. *Modest: Men and Women Clothed in the Gospel.* Adelphi, MD: Cruciform Press, 2012.

DeMoss, Nancy Leigh. *The Look: Does God Really Care What I Wear?* Buchanan, MI: Revive Our Hearts, 2003.

Gresh, Dannah. *Secret Keeper: The Delicate Power of Modesty.* Moody, 2005.

Mohler, Mary K. *Modeling Modesty.* Louisville, KY: Southern Baptist Theological Seminary, 2008.

Peace, Martha and Kent Keller. *Modesty: More Than a Change of Clothes*. Phillipsburg, NJ: P&R Publishing Company, 2015.

Pollard, Jeff. *Christian Modesty and the Public Undressing of America.* Pensacola, FL: Mt Zion Publications, 1999.

Spinney, Robert G. *Dressed to Kill: Thinking Biblically About Modest and Immodest Clothing.* Hartsville, TN: Tulip Books, 2007. [Note: If I could only recommend one thing on modesty, it would be this 29-page booklet.]

Vaughan, David and Diane. *The Beauty of Modesty: Cultivating Virtue in the Face of a Vulgar Culture.* Nashville, TN: Cumberland House Publishing, 2005.

Christian Literature on Modesty (Historic)

Alsop, Vincent. "What Distance Ought We to Keep, in Following the Strange Fashions of Apparel Which Come Up in the Days Wherein We Live?" in *Puritan Sermons 1659-1689* (Richard Owen Roberts, Publishers).

Baxter, Richard. "Christian Ethics" in *The Practical Works of Richard Baxter.*

Law, William. *A Serious Call to a Devout and Holy Life.*

Newton, John. "On Female Dress" in *The Works of John Newton, Volume 6.* Carlisle, PA: Banner of Truth, 1985 [1820]. It can also be found online at http://www.gracegems.org/Newton/130.htm. A slightly different version can be found online at https://books.google.com/books?id=AoQxAQAAMAAJ&printsec=frontcover#v=onepage&q&f=false

Wesley, John. "On Dress" in *The Works of John Wesley.* Grand Rapids, MI: Baker, 1979 [1872].

See also the following recent publications which contain substantial material from writers of the past:

Free Grace Broadcaster, Issue 216 (Summer 2011). *Modest Apparel*. Pensacola, FL: Chapel Library, 2011. It has excerpts from A. W. Pink, John Bunyan, Vincent Alsop, Richard Baxter and C. H. Spurgeon.

Vaughan, David and Diane. *The Beauty of Modesty: Cultivating Virtue in the Face of a Vulgar Culture.* Nashville, TN: Cumberland House Publishing, 2005. It has an appendix with excerpts from Tertullian, Ambrose, Martin Luther, Zacharius Ursinus, Thomas Aquinas, John Newton, Robert Hall, John Wesley, Jeremy Taylor, William Law, Henry Bullinger, James Durham, Thomas Watson, Robert Leighton, Ezekiel Hopkins and John Calvin.

Sexuality and Gender Differences

Arterburn, Stephen, Fred Stoeker and Mike Yorkey. *Every Man's Battle: Winning the War on Sexual Temptation One Victory at a Time.* Colorado Springs, CO: WaterBrook Press, 2009.

Arthur, Kay. *Sex... According to God.* Colorado Springs, CO: WaterBrook Press, 2002.

Dunn, Alan. *Gospel Intimacy in a Godly Marriage.* North Bergen, NJ: Pillar and Ground Publications, 2009.

Elliot, Elizabeth. *Let Me Be a Woman: Notes to My Daughter on the Meaning of Womanhood.* Wheaton, IL: Tyndale, 1976.

Ethridge, Shannon. *Every Woman's Battle.* Colorado Springs, CO: WaterBrook Press, 2003.

Feldhahn, Shaunti. *For Women Only: What You Need to Know about the Inner Lives of Men.* Multnomah, 2004.

Harris, Josh. *Sex Is Not the Problem (Lust Is): Sexual Purity in a Lust-Saturated World.* Colorado Springs, CO: Multnomah Books, 2003.

Mahaney, Carolyn and Nicole. *Girl Talk: Mother-Daughter Conversations on Biblical Womanhood.* Crossway Books, 2005.

Mbewe, Conrad. *Maintaining Sexual Purity (in a Sexually Permissive Society).* Lusaka, Zambia: Evergreen Publishers, 2009.

Piper, John and Wayne Grudem, ed. *Recovering Biblical Manhood and Womanhood: A Response to Evangelical Feminism.* Wheaton, IL: Crossway Books, 1991. [See especially the chapter "Biological Basis for Gender-Specific Behavior" by Gregg Johnson.]

Sax, Leonard. *Why Gender Matters: What Parents and Teachers Need to Know about the Emerging Science of Sex Differences.* Doubleday, 2005.

Shalit, Wendy. *Girls Gone MILD: Young Women Reclaim Self-Respect and Find It's Not Bad to Be Good.* New York: Random House, 2007.

Miscellaneous

DeMoss, Nancy Leigh. *Becoming a Woman of Discretion in a Sensual World.* Buchanan, MI: Revive Our Hearts, 2003.

El Guindi, Fadwa. *Veil: Modesty, Privacy and Resistance.* Berg, 1999.

Mahaney, C. J. and John Piper. *Worldliness: Resisting the Seduction of a Fallen World.* Crossway, 2008.

Shalit, Wendy. *A Return to Modesty: Discovering the Lost Virtue.* Free Press, 2014. [Note: The cover on the original edition of 1999 leaves much to be desired in the way of modesty. Last year they reprinted it with a much more appropriate cover so I suggest making sure you get the 2014 edition.]

Spiegel, James S. *How to Be Good in a World Gone Bad.* Grand Rapids, MI: Kregel Publications, 2004.

Scripture Index

OLD TESTAMENT

Song of Solomon

Isaiah

Jeremiah

Lamentations

Ezekiel

Hosea

Amos

Micah

Nahum

Zechariah

NEW TESTAMENT

Also Available
from

Christian Focus Publications

YOUR FUTURE
'OTHER HALF'
It matters whom you marry

Rebecca VanDoodewaard

ISBN 978-1-78191-298-0

Your Future 'Other Half'

It matters whom you marry

REBECCA VANDOODEWAARD

Rebecca Vandoodewaard of *The Christian Pundit* blogsite gives Biblical advice for women who are in a relationship, who wish to be in a relationship, or who struggle in an imperfect marriage by addressing the spiritual, emotional, mental, physical and relational effects of intimacy and answering questions for the single or married such as: Where does love fit in? and, How do I fit in?

With kindness and truth woven together, she unpacks the long-term mental, emotional, physical and spiritual impact of marriage. This book is a valuable and much needed resource for women.

Melissa B. Kruger,
Conference speaker, Women's Ministry Coordinator, Uptown Church, Charlotte, North Carolina

Finally, a book for the woman wondering if she has found the right man for a life-long commitment... This book is a must read for any woman thinking about marriage, in a marriage now, or helping others towards a life-long biblical romance that echoes the love of Christ for His Bride and her joyous "Yes!" to Him. Buy it! Read it! Use it! I know I will.

Jani Ortlund
Author of *Fearlessly Feminine* and other books, speaker, wife of Ray Ortlund, Executive Vice President, Renewal Ministries, Franklin, Tennessee

Rebecca VanDoodewaard is a freelance editor. Her husband, William, is ordained in the Associate Reformed Presbyterian Church in Grand Rapids, Michigan. Until recently they blogged together at thechristianpundit.org

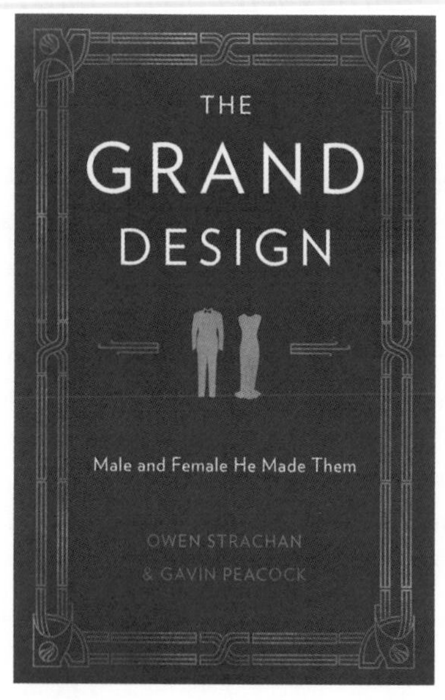

ISBN 978-1-78191-764-0

The Grand Design

Male and Female He Made Them

Owen Strachan and Gavin Peacock

The world has gone gray-fuzzy, blurry, gender-neutral gray. In a secularist culture, many people today are confused about what it means to be a man or a woman. Even the church struggles to understand the meaning of manhood and womanhood. In The Grand Design, Owen Strachan and Gavin Peacock clear away the confusion and open up the Scriptures. They show that the gospel frees us to behold the unity and distinctiveness of the sexes. In Christ, we have a script for our lives. Doxology, we discover, is in the details.

We live in an age characterized by confusion on gender and sexuality ... Strachan and Peacock have provided a careful and faithful account of Scripture's vision for sexuality and gender. This book is urgently needed.

R. Albert Mohler, Jr.

President, The Southern Baptist Theological Seminary, Louisville, Kentucky

Owen Strachan is the president of the Council on Biblical Manhood & Womanhood and Associate Professor of Christian Theology at Midwestern Baptist Theological Seminary in Kansas City, Missouri.

Gavin Peacock played for Chelsea Football Club. He is now Director of International Outreach for the Council on Biblical Manhood & Womanhood, and serves as a pastor at Calvary Grace Church in Calgary, Alberta.

ISBN 978-1-84550-775-6

The Envy of Eve

Finding Contentment in a Covetous world

MELISSA B. KRUGER

What's truly at the heart of our desires?

The Envy of Eve guides readers to understand how desires grow into covetousness and what happens when this sin takes power in our hearts. Covetousness chokes out the fruit of the Spirit in our lives, allowing discontentment to bloom. The key to overcoming is to get to the root of our problem: unbelief-a mistrust of God's sovereignty and goodness. An ideal resource for deeper study or group discussion.

With empathy and grounded biblical insight, Melissa Kruger shows us the path to abiding joy amidst life's varied 'ups' and 'downs'."

Lydia Brownback
Author of *Contentment*, Wheaton, Illinois

With I've-been-there understanding and been-in-the-Word insight, Melissa B. Kruger helps us to look beneath the surface of our discontent, exposing our covetous hearts to the healing light of God's Word.

Nancy Guthrie
Author of *Seeing Jesus in the Old Testament Bible Study Series*

Melissa B. Kruger serves as Women's Ministry Coordinator at Uptown Church in Charlotte, North Carolina. Her husband, Michael J. Kruger, is the president of Reformed Theological Seminary in Charlotte. She is an author and is a speaker at various Christian conferences across the United States.

ISBN 978-1-78191-584-4

And Then He Knew Her

A Biblical View of Sex

Adrian and Celia Reynolds

Do we really need a book about sex? In a world seemingly obsessed, should this be a subject that stays 'in the bedroom'? Adrian and Celia Reynolds explore what the Bible teaches about sex. What is sex for? Why is it important? And why does it belong in marriage? Taking on board these simple truths and applying these realities to your own life will ensure that your view of sex is no more and no less than God intends.

Adrian and Celia Reynolds have clearly met their aim to introduce the subject of sex in a biblical, brief and direct way. It's a wonderfully logical and helpful book. It's easy to read, but certainly not lightweight in content.

In our sex saturated society this excellent little volume could be profitably passed on to those who want a clearer understanding of what the Bible teaches about God's good gift of sex … it will encorage any reader, married or single, to think carefully about their own attitude to sex, ensuring that it's no more and no less than our Creator intends.

Evangelicals Now

Adrian Reynolds is Director of Ministry of the Proclamation Trust and also serves as associate minister at East London Tabernacle Baptist Church, London.

Celia Reynolds tutors students for the Cornhill Training Course, serves in the church and also works locally as a Community Parent. Along with husband Adrian they run conferences for and work with married couples.

Christian Focus Publications

Our mission statement –

STAYING FAITHFUL
In dependence upon God we seek to impact the world through literature faithful to His infallible Word, the Bible. Our aim is to ensure that the Lord Jesus Christ is presented as the only hope to obtain forgiveness of sin, live a useful life and look forward to heaven with Him.

Our books are published in four imprints:

CHRISTIAN FOCUS

Popular works including biographies, commentaries, basic doctrine and Christian living.

CHRISTIAN HERITAGE

Books representing some of the best material from the rich heritage of the church.

MENTOR

Books written at a level suitable for Bible College and seminary students, pastors, and other serious readers. The imprint includes commentaries, doctrinal studies, examination of current issues and church history.

CF4•K

Children's books for quality Bible teaching and for all age groups: Sunday school curriculum, puzzle and activity books; personal and family devotional titles, biographies and inspirational stories – Because you are never too young to know Jesus!

Christian Focus Publications Ltd,
Geanies House, Fearn, Ross-shire,
IV20 1TW, Scotland, United Kingdom.
www.christianfocus.com